Estate Planning for Everyone

Estate Planning
The whole truth —

Richard S. Ziegler
and Patrick F. Flaherty

for Everyone
from planning to probate

New Revised Edition

PREMIER PUBLISHING CO.
Minneapolis, Minnesota

Previously published by
HARPER & ROW, PUBLISHERS
Cambridge, Hagerstown, Philadelphia, San Francisco,
London, Mexico City, São Paulo, Sydney

1817

Estate Planning for Everyone
ERRATA

Chap. 6, pp. 54 & 55, and
Tables 1 and 2:

The Federal Unified Credit for 1982 and 1983 is $62,800 and $79,300 respectively, and not $64,000 and $77,300 as printed in the tables.

Chap. 6, p. 60, line 26:

In the example given, the Federal Estate Tax should be $52,200, not $65,400.

Copyright © 1972, by Richard S. Ziegler & Patrick F. Flaherty

Copyright © 1981, by Richard S. Ziegler & Patrick F. Flaherty

Copyright © 1982, by Richard S. Ziegler & Patrick F. Flaherty

All rights reserved. Printed in the United States of America. No part of this book may be used or reproduced in any manner whatsoever without written permission except in the case of brief quotations embodied in critical articles and reviews. For information address Premier Publishing Co., 1200 Pillsbury Center, Minneapolis, MN 55402. Previously published in the United States by Harper & Row, Publishers, Inc., New York, N.Y., and in Canada by Fitzhenry & Whiteside Limited, Toronto.

Library of Congress Catalog No. 82-80173

Ziegler, Richard S. and Patrick F. Flaherty
    Estate Planning for Everyone.

ISBN 0-942622-00-6

Contents

     Authors' note   vii

1. Your estate   1

2. Your will   9

3. What is probate?   17

4. The truth about joint tenancy   25

5. Trusts   34

6. Estate and inheritance taxes   52

7. Estate planning   69

8. The role of the lawyer and estate planning aides   78

9. Choosing trustees and estate administrators   86

10. Sample plans   92

     In conclusion   120

     Estate inventory worksheets   121

     Glossary   133

     Index   135

Authors' note

This is the decade of the '80s. Inflation seems to have become a way of life. Attitudes are changing. Goals are changing. Investments are changing. Values are changing. But one thing has not changed—the need to keep your estate plan up to date. In fact, now more than ever, thinking people want to do everything they can to make sure their affairs are in proper order.

This is the new revised edition of *Estate Planning for Everyone*. We have expanded several sections to provide more specific counsel, have updated the sample estate plans, and included information to show you how to take advantage of the sweeping changes resulting from the Economic Recovery Tax Act of 1981. This legislation makes it essential for you to review your personal and your family's estate planning. Failure to do so may result in your paying higher taxes while you live and your heirs doing so after you die.

Our book is designed as a guide to help you plan your estate to achieve long-term goals, to save on taxes, and to assure greater protection of assets for family security and well-being. It explains legal terms and concepts in a way that is easy to read and understand. It takes the mystery out of estate planning.

The text reflects our personal experiences as estate planning attorneys. Some details of our advice may vary in different states, but the principles are applicable across the country. In the pages that follow, you will learn why we believe that a properly planned estate is one of the best gifts any man or woman can leave his or her heirs.

Richard S. Ziegler and Patrick F. Flaherty

1

Your estate
- **HOW PROPERTY IS HELD**
- **WHAT HAPPENS TO IT WHEN YOU DIE**

Estate planning is one of the most important responsibilities an individual has. It is the development of a plan to manage and dispose of the assets and liabilities you leave at death in a way best suited to the needs of your beneficiaries.

Most estates involve a home, savings, investments, life insurance, and personal belongings. Wise estate planning can enable you, your family, and your other beneficiaries to retain a greater share of your estate by providing for its proper management and enjoyment and minimizing the erosion of it by taxes.

You are richer than you think. The average middle-class American owns a car, a home, and furnishings, and has some savings, life insurance, and pension benefits. Others may have investments in real estate, stocks and bonds, or an interest in a business such as a small corporation, partnership, or proprietorship. The value of many of these investments will fluctuate depending on supply and demand. Your hope, of course, is that they will increase in value and will also provide income. Over the years, the total estates of many families will grow to a sizable sum. Wise estate planning will not only help to boost the worth of your estate, but can also keep taxes at a more reasonable level.

Whatever the form of your wealth, you have silent partners: the federal government and, often, state and local authorities. They levy taxes on money when you receive it and when you leave it.

In recent years, two things have become major concerns for everyone who owns anything: inflation and taxes. Proper financial planning can be beneficial in dealing with both problems. There are limits to what one person can do about inflation, but there are many things you can do about the costs and problems of transferring the things you own to your family and loved ones at your death.

This book discusses, in a general way, questions about wills, probate, taxes, legal fees, and many of the complications involved in death and inheritance. This information will not make you an estate planner or financial adviser, but it will make you aware of the problems and help you to understand the methods you can use to solve them and judge the competency of your advisers.

This is not a "do-it-yourself" book, because the business of estate planning is too important to be left to the untrained. You get no second chance to come back and correct your mistakes.

The single most important step in estate planning is to make a will. This last testament serves two basic purposes: to set down, in writing, how you wish your property to be distributed after your death and who you want to do the job.

When there's no will, your estate will be distributed according to the laws of the state in which you live, not as you may want. The lack of a will can be difficult for your heirs and lead to unforeseen results and unnecessary taxes and expenses.

WHAT IS PROPERTY?

The technical name for things that people acquire is *property*. This general term means anything capable of being owned: real estate, personal belongings, automobiles, clothing, household furnishings, savings, investments, and so on.

Specifically, property can be divided into two categories:

1. Real estate, which includes not only land but also buildings and other fixtures permanently attached to it.
2. Personal property, of which there are two types:
   a. *Tangible:* that which you can touch, such as a car, clothing, or a painting.
   b. *Intangible:* that which represents ownership, such as a stock certificate or savings account.

OWNERSHIP OF PROPERTY To own property means to possess or hold it and to enjoy or control its private use. There are several different ways in which owners hold their property. Each is treated differently at the owner's death.

The following are common ways of holding property:

1. *In Your Own Name.* Usually, we think of property as being held in an individual's own name. This is sometimes referred to as "sole-name" ownership. No one else has any interest in the property.

Often, sole-name ownership involves some kind of registration in which your name is actually associated with the property in a formal manner. If you buy a piece of real estate, you will receive a deed on which your name will appear as the owner. If the deed is recorded, the property rolls in the county in which the property is located will list your name as the owner, and a local unit of government will recognize this possession by levying taxes and sending you the bill.

Other kinds of investment property are also subject to sole-name ownership and formal registration. For example, the owner's name will be inserted on the certificate of shares of stock or registered bonds of a business corporation and will also be shown on the books and records of the company.

Some kinds of sole-name ownership do not involve formal registration, so that possession of such property becomes your only evidence of ownership. This is usually the case when you purchase a painting or receive a gift of cash.

2. *Ownership with Others.* Sometimes shared ownership may be necessary and desirable. Such situations occur when ownership involves property that cannot be divided without destroying its function. Examples are a piece of real estate that cannot be divided easily: for example, a homestead or property owned by two or more individuals who plan to use it in a business venture such as a partnership.

Often, shared ownership is subject to a written agreement, and in some cases is submitted to formal registration.

The two most common forms of ownership with others are *joint tenancy* and *tenancy in common*. Their effects are more complex and far reaching than you may realize. Here's what each term means:

JOINT TENANCY With this arrangement, two or more individuals own an undivided portion of the property's total value. If there are two joint tenants, each owns an undivided half; if three, each owns an undivided third; and so on. This type of ownership is the subject of a separate chapter.

In legal terms, "undivided portion" means that there is no identification of any joint tenant with any specific portion of the property. Each interest covers the whole. Each tenant owns a fraction of the entire value, usually in proportion to the original investment.

In the event of the death of one of the joint tenants, his or her entire interest in the property automatically goes to the surviving joint tenant or tenants. This is called *right of survivorship*. When we say *automatically*, we mean that this process of transfer takes place without reference to the deceased joint tenant's will or the probate of that will. The deceased joint tenant's will, if he or she has one, has absolutely *no effect* on the joint tenancy property. The reason why so many property owners use joint tenancy is to facilitate the transfer of property to a surviving joint tenant (most often a spouse or other family member) in the event of death without the necessity of probate. Joint tenancy must be created by a *writing* which mentions the right of survivorship.

TENANCY IN COMMON This is exactly like joint tenancy except that there is no right of survivorship or automatic transfer at death. If two persons own a piece of real estate as tenants in common, and one of them dies, the share of the property belonging to the deceased tenant in common passes by means of his or her will, or if there is no will, according to applicable state laws. Generally, each cotenant's share of the property is treated as though it were owned separately. For example, if spouses hold property as tenants in common, the survivor does not automatically receive the deceased spouse's share. The deceased spouse's share is subject to probate. The surviving spouse must depend on a will or state law establishing a spouse's share. These laws vary from state to state and the size of the share may depend on how many children also survive.

Here are some additional types of property ownership:

TENANCY BY THE ENTIRETIES is a particular kind of joint tenancy between spouses. It cannot be changed unless both spouses agree. Some states do not recognize this kind of holding.

PARTNERSHIP An oral or written understanding underlies this kind of ownership. Commonly, it's a combination of two or more individuals, each contributing property (money, real estate, or the like) and agreeing that it will be used in a certain manner, usually in a business venture.

Unless the partnership agreement provides otherwise, at the death of one owner the partnership will terminate and the deceased partner's share of the assets will be distributed in accordance with his will or applicable state laws in a probate proceeding.

To be in a partnership without a specific, written agreement is pure folly. Misunderstandings can arise when there are no clearly defined provisions. Even if you and your partners get along fine while you are alive, the lack of a written statement can cause problems at death.

In all partnerships, spell out the responsibilities of ownership, preferably with the aid of an attorney.

COMMUNITY PROPERTY In certain states, the laws provide that property acquired during marriage by means other than gift or inheritance is owned equally by husband and wife. With some exceptions, when one spouse dies, his or her estate consists of one half of these community property assets.

At present, community property states are Arizona, California, Idaho, Louisiana, Nevada, New Mexico, Texas, and Washington. Similar laws in Hawaii, Michigan, Nebraska, Oklahoma, and Oregon have been repealed.

The historical basis for community property ownership is found in Spanish, Mexican, and French law. It's a lot like having a marital partnership. By law, the man is the administrator, but both persons have the same interest in all property and in all income generated by either party's labor. At death, the estate is divided in half.

There are exceptions in which separate or "noncommunity" property is allowed even though one's legal residence may be in a community property state. Here are examples:

- Any assets acquired by either party before marriage. Afterward, the income, profits, and improvements relating to such property may be considered community property.
- Gifts or inheritance, even during the marriage.
- Earnings of a wife while she is separated from her husband (in some states only).
- Compensation received by an injured partner.

People residing in community property states should be aware of three things:

a. *The importance of accurate records,* especially of property acquired in a noncommunity property state. Recognizing that there may be confusion as to who owns what, these states have statutes that, in effect, say that when there's doubt as to ownership, the property must be considered jointly owned.

b. *Many community property states are retirement areas to which older people move.* Frequently, these retirees have accumulated most of their wealth in noncommunity, common-law states. Generally, such assets do not become joint property at change of residence, but this is not always true.

In California, for instance, the law states that unless certain legal precautions are taken, a surviving spouse may claim the absolute right to inherit half of the decedent's estate. This holds regardless of whether such assets were acquired in a noncommunity property state and even though the decedent may have planned (but not in writing) to leave them to someone else.

c. *The community property state provisions may apply even if the parties later move to a noncommunity property state or foreign country.*

Advice: If you are going to move to or from a community property state, see a lawyer immediately to be sure that your estate plan fulfills your objectives under the law of your new home.

3. *Subject to Beneficiary Designation.* The transfer at death takes place according to a "beneficiary designation." It is automatic and does not depend on a will or probate.

With life insurance, for example, the owner of the policy names one or more persons or organizations to receive the proceeds at the owner's death. When the policyholder dies, the insurance company makes the payment directly to the beneficiary or beneficiaries as stated in the policy's beneficiary provisions.

This procedure is also followed with the proceeds of most pension and profit-sharing plans. If the employee dies before retirement, the benefits are paid as designated by the individual employee.

Note that unless specifically made payable to the estate, such properties do *not* pass through the deceased's estate and are not subject to the terms of a will or, when there is no will, to the requirements of state laws.

4. Held in Trust. This type of ownership is discussed in detail later, but broadly speaking, a trust is a written agreement that puts property under the direction of a trustee. At some future time, often beyond the life of the person establishing the trust, the agreement is terminated and the property involved distributed to the designated beneficiary or beneficiaries.

Holding property in trust is a means of ownership, similar to the ownership of an insurance policy in that the property is ultimately distributed to beneficiaries designated by the one establishing the trust and is not usually subject to the terms of that person's will or the probate process. Many trusts involve tax savings.

ACQUISITION OF PROPERTY

Property is acquired in different ways:
- With savings, by purchase alone, or in partnership with others.
- With profits on investments.
- On credit such as a mortgage.
- Through gifts and/or inheritances.

As you'll learn in the chapters ahead, there are many ways to plan your estate to make the disposition of property easier and less expensive, and the property itself less heavily taxed.

Remember

1. Ownership means *possession* and *control of enjoyment*.
2. Property is either *real* or *personal*.
3. Personal property is either *tangible* or *intangible*.
4. Property may be owned alone (sole name) or with others.
5. Shared ownership means: tenancy in common, joint tenancy (with right of survivorship), tenancy by the entireties, partnership, community property.
6. Insurance and retirement rights are often subject to beneficiary designation.
7. Property held in trust passes according to a written trust document.
8. Property passes at the death of the owner in accordance with a will, probate laws, right of survivorship, beneficiary designation, or the terms of a trust—it all depends on how it is held.

2

Your will

How often the question is asked: "Why do I need an attorney to help me write a will? I know what I want." The answer is simple: You do not need an attorney to help you write your will. You can do it yourself. But people who do can create serious problems causing their heirs financial loss.

There's the story about the man who wrote his own will and merely said, "I leave everything to Mom." What could be clearer? It seemed, however, he had had the habit during his lifetime of referring to his wife as "Mom," and to complicate matters, he was survived by his wife and his mother.

There is a toast each year at the British Bar Convention. It is to the person who prepares his own will. So often litigation results from homemade wills, and litigation, of course, is what lawyers thrive on.

A VALID WILL

A will has to comply with the laws of the state within which the person making the will resides at the time it is signed. The laws of the various states are not uniform. But as a general principle, it can be said that in most states a will is valid if it is signed by one of legal age before two witnesses of legal age and if at the time it is so signed the person making the will declares in the presence of the witnesses that the instrument is his last will and testament and he wants them to act as witnesses to his will. He then signs the will and the witnesses then sign, all in the presence of each other. Normally, only the original of the will is signed, for the reason that if it is revoked or changed in the future, there is only one original instrument to look for.

Most states have laws that provide that a will validly entered into by a person in another state will be recognized in the state within which the person making the will dies even if that state's law of execution is different.

A properly drawn will should dispose of everything. A person's assets change during his lifetime. It is very unusual for a person to die with exactly the same assets he owned at the time he made his will. It generally is not good technique to designate specific assets to specific beneficiaries. For instance, if you want to give a son stock in XYZ corporation worth $5,000, it would be better to give him a specific amount of $5,000. You may not own any shares of XYZ corporation when you die.

There are exceptions to the rule. For instance, you have a business. This item might be mentioned specifically.

All properly prepared wills have what is called a residuary clause. A residuary clause is one that, after you have designated certain specific items or amounts to go to certain persons, states: "I give and devise all of the rest, residue, and remainder of my estate of whatever kind and whatsoever nature to my _____ ." Or the residuary clause might read: "I give and devise all of the rest, residue, and remainder of my estate 10% thereof to my son, John, if he survives me and if he does not survive me then to his children who do survive me by right of representation: 10% thereof to my daughter, Mary," etc.

There are, of course, many, many different ways of writing wills. A well-drafted will provides for all contingencies, particularly the contingency of what is to happen in the event that the person you want to have some portion of your estate does not survive you. Sometimes a special survival provision is in the will to the effect that in order for a person to take under your will, he or she must survive you by a certain period of time—e.g., thirty days.

There oftentimes is what is called the simultaneous death clause, a clause that provides for what is to happen if you and your spouse die under such circumstances that it is not possible to determine which of you died first—for instance, if you were both killed in an airplane accident. The clause would provide a presumption that one survived the other—and the decision as to which is presumed to survive probably would be based on tax considerations.

An important part of a will is the tax clause—the clause that provides for payment of the death taxes, if any. Of major concern in many cases is the structuring of language in the tax clause of a will to make sure the assets are left in such a way as to minimize federal estate taxes and state inheritance or estate taxes.

One of the most important parts of a will is that which nominates the person or organization that is to act as your personal representative (in some states referred to as the executor). Your personal representative can be anyone of legal age or it can be a professional such as a bank or trust company authorized by law to act as such (see Chapter 9).

In many instances, a will is the most important document a person ever signs. No thinking person would want to take a chance on such an important document being defective, with the possible result that the persons you intended to receive your wealth do not get it.

WHO SHOULD BE WITNESSES TO A WILL?

If you have been asked to be a witness to someone's will, chances are you are not a beneficiary in the will. Though many states have now changed their laws so that a witness to a will can also be a beneficiary in the will, there are still many state laws that specifically provide that a witness to a will either takes nothing under the will or that the share of the witness is limited to the amount the witness would have received if the person died without a will—and often this is nothing.

Even in states that allow witnesses to take under the will, it is better procedure to have persons witness the will that are not in any way beneficiaries under the will. Generally, the lawyer who prepares a will acts as one of the witnesses. In most states the witnesses have to be of legal age—age eighteen in some states, age twenty-one in others.

It is a good idea for the witnesses to the will to be younger than the person signing the will. The obvious reason for this is that in case of disputes after the death of the one signing the will, it is most helpful if the person who witnessed the will is alive and able to testify as to what went on at the time the will was signed.

WHAT MAKES A WILL INVALID?

A will that is not signed and properly witnessed is invalid. Assuming the will has been properly signed and witnessed and disposes of all assets, it still may be invalidated, at least in part, if:

1. It violates certain statutory rights of the maker's heirs at law. For instance, in most states, a surviving spouse—unless during the lifetime of the person whose will is being challenged that spouse properly waived his or her statutory rights—will be entitled to certain sums out of the estate of the deceased spouse, generally from one third to one half of the estate.
2. It can be established that the will was procured by fraud or the decendent was subject to undue influence—fraud and undue influence are very closely related in will contest litigation.
3. It can be established that the decedent was not competent at the time the will was signed. Competency to make a valid last will and testament is generally not the same competency as is required in signing, for instance, a complicated contract. In most states, all that really is necessary to determine that the person signing the will was competent is to establish that that person knew the objects of his or her bounty, had a general idea of the extent of his or her wealth, and at the time the instrument was signed intended that the persons designated in the instrument be the ones to receive his or her wealth.

BUT IT'S NOT FAIR

How often we hear omitted heirs say that the will was not fair. Fairness hasn't a thing to do with it. If the person signing the will was of sound and disposing mind at the time of signing, was not under any undue influence, and the will was validly signed and witnessed, it will be honored by the court, even though the judge might agree that it was not fair.

Sometimes persons who take care of and have genuine regard for a particular person are not adequately provided for in that person's will. Relief can be achieved by making a claim in the estate of the deceased person for services rendered, but oftentimes those claims are difficult to prove and if proved, the amount received does not adequately compensate the omitted person for all of his or her efforts.

Persons of wealth have been known to lead others on with such statements as: "Don't worry; you will be taken care of in my will." But then, when that person dies, the promise has not been fulfilled in the will. Perhaps the promise was false. Perhaps late in life something happened whereby the person was offended, often inadvertently or mistakenly, and the will was changed to cut out a beneficiary. In most states, even if the decedent was mistaken about a situation that caused him or her to change the will and eliminate a particular beneficiary, the courts still will honor the document and that beneficiary will take only what the will provides, if anything.

HOW DO I CHANGE MY WILL?

One can change a will as many times as one wants. It is only the will that is in effect at the time of death that controls. If the change is a short one, it can be accomplished by what is called a codicil. The word "codicil" really means "amendment."

But remember, the codicil has to be signed with the same formality as a will. Under no circumstances should a valid will, after it has been properly signed and witnessed, be scratched out, modified, or in any other way changed, because to do so will perhaps invalidate the whole instrument or, as a bare minimum, result in confusion that may require court interpretations or maybe even litigation.

STATUTORY RIGHTS — PREMARITAL AGREEMENTS

As stated above, most surviving spouses have certain statutory rights in the decedent's estate unless during the decedent's lifetime the surviving spouse waived his or her rights.

How can these rights be waived? Often they are waived by what is called an "antenuptial" or "premarital" agreement. For instance, it is not uncommon for parties to a second marriage, particularly when both have families from prior marriages, to enter into a premarital agreement whereby, in consideration of the pending marriage, each waives statutory rights in the property of the other, to the end that if either dies, property can be left to whomever he or she chooses without any requirement to comply with statutory provisions for a surviving spouse.

These agreements sometimes are valid only if they are entered into prior to marriage. Generally, the parties to the antenuptial agreement have to make a full disclosure to each other of the extent of their assets. Also, it is best if the parties to the agreement are represented by different lawyers.

Antenuptial agreements are awkward. They are entered into at a time when love is in the air and the parties to the contract are often planning their marriage. Affirming trust in each other, they state that all they want from each other is love and not property.

It is not uncommon, even though an antenuptial agreement has been entered into, to also have a waiver of statutory rights signed at the same time wills are prepared for the newlyweds. It is sort of "frosting on the cake." It generally is not necessary that consents to new wills be signed.

After marriage, if the parties have failed to sign a premarital agreement, it still is possible in certain states for them to enter into a valid postnuptial agreement; but after the marriage, there is obviously not the same incentive for the spouse with few assets to sign away any of his or her rights to the more substantial assets of the other spouse.

In some states, antenuptial agreements can also provide for waiver of alimony, support, and property settlement if the marriage does not work out and ends in divorce. In fact, such agreements are sometimes used in sophisticated "live-in lover" situations.

HANDWRITTEN WILLS

There are states where a person can write out and sign, without any witnesses, a valid will if he does it all in his own handwriting. Not many states still recognize such so-called holographic wills, however.

Perhaps the most famous situation of this kind involved Howard Hughes. At last count, there were over thirty alleged holographic wills by Howard Hughes! None of them have been determined to be valid.

The authors are totally opposed to holographic wills. For instance, a person is in the hospital, upset because none of his relatives are visiting him, and decides to leave everything to his nurse, who is taking such good care of him. The patient writes out a will accordingly and forgets about it. Five years later he dies, and the writing turns up, leaving everything to the nurse. Not fair, perhaps, but it would control if the state the person lived in honored holographic wills.

A will is a very serious document and in the judgment of the authors it should be signed before witnesses with certain formalities accomplished at the time of signing.

Understand that a will can be handwritten as well as typewritten. A holographic will is one that is totally handwritten and signed by the person making the will and without witnesses. A handwritten will signed before two witnesses who also signed the document, all in the presence of each other, is just as good as a typewritten instrument properly signed and witnessed.

There are other examples of famous handwritten wills besides the Howard Hughes fiasco. There is the story about the farmer whose tractor tipped over on him; knowing he was going to die, he managed to scratch out on the fender of the tractor that he left everything to his wife. That was accomplished in a state that allowed holographic wills and the fender of the tractor was then duly admitted to probate.

Or take the actual incident of the person who, choking on his food in a restaurant, had the presence to scratch his will on a napkin before the required witnesses, and then he died. The napkin was duly admitted to probate as a valid last will and testament.

DOES A WILL AVOID PROBATE?

For some reason, many people think that a valid will eliminates probate. It does not. A valid will does assure that the designated persons will receive the estate. Most important, it designates who is to handle the decedent's affairs. (See Chapter 3: "What is probate?")

IF I HAVE EVERYTHING IN JOINT TENANCY, WHY DO I NEED A WILL?

You never know who is going to survive. If you have everything in joint tenancy with your spouse and your spouse dies a few minutes before you, then it is all yours and you should have a will to designate what is to happen in that event. See Chapter 4: "The Truth About Joint Tenancy."

WHERE SHOULD I KEEP MY WILL?

The answer to this is: a safe place. We usually recommend that it be put in a safe-deposit box. It is possible that after death, under the laws of your state your safe-deposit box may be sealed until the local officials can inventory its contents to make sure that all the assets of the deceased person are reported for death-tax purposes. This usually produces little or no delay or inconvenience to the administration of the estate. An appointment for the official inventory can be easily arranged to coincide with a visit to the safe-deposit box by the nominated personal representative, attorney and interested family members. At the conclusion of the inventory, the original will, if found in the box, is released to the custody of the nominated personal representative or delivered to the probate court so that probate may be commenced. Of course, a copy of the will should be retained by the testator for easy reference and he or she should leave information as to where the original can be found. The testator's attorney usually retains only a copy of the will.

3

What is probate?

The word *"probate"* strikes fear in the hearts of those who hear it, yet few people understand the term. Writers have become rich trying to tell people how to avoid it, and property owners go to great lengths to stay away from it. All too often, attempts to avoid probate have resulted in the wrong people receiving property and the right ones having to pay heavy and unnecessary estate and inheritance taxes.

Probate is not a monster created by unscrupulous lawyers and fostered by corrupt judges. It is a valid legal process and, for that reason, has lasted for centuries.

The term *probate* is generally used to signify an important part of a court system that exists in the fifty states and in all countries of the free world. It refers to the process that governs the administration and distribution of property belonging to persons who have died. It also means the enforcement of the terms of a person's last will or ensuring adherence to laws concerning the distribution of property for a person who has died without a will.

To the layman, probate may appear to be a slow, cumbersome, and expensive process. For that reason, some people argue that it should be updated and simplified. We agree wholeheartedly. In fact, probate has already been revised in many states. However, no one with any real knowledge of the law governing estates wants the system to be abolished. It works and has proven a powerful legal safeguard for millions of people.

Probate property is real estate, securities, jewelry, automobiles, art, coins, and other assets held in the name of an individual *alone*.

There is no predetermination by trust, joint tenancy, or beneficiary as to how the property will pass at death.

After demise, the distribution of the property is made in accordance with a will if the owner dies with a valid last testament. When there is no acceptable will, the estate passes by what is known as "intestate" law under which the pattern of distribution is dictated by statute.

With or without a will, every estate held by a person in his own name must go through probate. What this means is that *everybody has a will whether or not he knows it*. If you are not prudent enough to prepare a last testament, the state provides a ready-made will under intestate law.

If you want your property to go to a specific individual, you should have a valid will (one properly drawn and accepted by the court). If you do not leave such a document, the court must act according to the law, which may require that your property be distributed in a manner entirely different from what you desire. The probate court, in effect, is a referee in the allocation of your estate, either in accordance with your will if you leave one or in accordance with state law if you die without a valid will. If you die without a will or your will is proved invalid and no relatives can be located, your property is forfeited to the state.

DEATH WITHOUT A WILL

Among Americans who die each year, more than 70 percent leave no will. Wives and single people are especially remiss in this area. Unfortunately, not leaving a will can have costly consequences.

If you die without a will and heirs survive you, your assets will be distributed by impersonal law under the jurisdiction of a personal representative appointed by the court. He must work within the narrow outlines of statutes designed to provide the greatest good for the greatest number of people. There's little room for sentiment, for following your wishes, or for making allocations according to need.

In most states, if one dies without a will the decedent's spouse will get one third to one half of the decedent's estate and the rest will be split among the children, regardless of their age or circumstances. The same percentage of a man's wealth will go to his seven-year-old son as to his married daughter, or to his affluent son as to his crippled daughter, whom he might have wanted to help to a greater extent.

If you die without a will and no spouse or children or grandchildren survive you, then most state laws will split your property among your parents or the survivor thereof, and if neither survives, then to your brothers and sisters—and if you have no surviving brothers or sisters or nieces and nephews, right on down the line until cousins, second cousins, etc., surface to inherit your wealth.

ROLE OF THE PROBATE COURT

The probate court acts as a referee and decision maker by answering pertinent questions and resolving conflicts of interpretation. In the case of a poorly worded will, the question might be: "What did the draftsman mean?" Or the heirs might ask: "Were the terms of the will procured by undue influence?"; "Was the person making the will of sound and disposing mind?"; "Are there indications that the person handling the estate has made a serious mistake or is guilty of embezzlement?"; "Who makes sure that the estate representative pays the taxes and just debts?"; or "How can a dispute over a debt be resolved?"

Although many probate court functions are more or less routine, there can be occasions when the answers to such questions will be significant to beneficiaries; one example is the decision of the court as to which assets should be sold to make the designated allocations of assets.

TIME AND COST OF PROBATE

The next important and often most alarming questions have to do with how long probate will take and how much it will cost.

Time There are no set answers on time. The length of a probate depends on the nature of the assets, tax problems, and the complexity of the legacies. Probates can take as little as one month if a summary proceeding (a short formal review under the court's jurisdiction) is held, or they can drag out for years if the estate is diverse, tax problems exist, or disputes occur.

Do not be alarmed at the prospect that probate may take as long as two years or more. That length of time is unusual, but it is not necessarily injurious. Often, long periods of probate can be used to secure tax advantages for the beneficiaries. This is because a probate estate is a separate taxpayer. But you should be fully informed by your lawyer as to "why" it is taking so long.

A probate can achieve tax savings in several ways: by delaying distributions to keep income in the estate, which may have a lower income tax rate than the eventual beneficiaries; or by "sprinkling"—a process whereby different sums are paid to different beneficiaries at different times. For example, allocating more income to children, who are subject to a low tax rate, than to a high-tax-bracket adult.

In spite of tax benefits that may be derived, most beneficiaries want to get things over with and push for quick completion of probate. Your attorney will tell you that ending probate promptly is usually best. When probate is protracted, there is a possibility that the Internal Revenue Service will rule that the estate was held open for an unreasonable time and thus may not be eligible for tax savings.

Cost In the past, the cost of probate was based strictly on the value of the estate. State bar associations often established a schedule of attorney fees expressed as a percentage of estate value: usually from 3 to 4 percent for estates under $500,000, and the dollar fees increasing with the size of the estate but constituting a smaller percentage of total value. Bar Association-mandated fee schedules are no longer used. Legal fees for probating estates are now most often based on the time it takes lawyers and their assistants (paralegals) to do the job. In a modern law office an attorney specializing in estate planning and probate law heads a team of lay assistants. The job is broken down into constituent parts, each part being delegated to a person who can best handle it for the least cost (least time charge). The attorney is the captain of the team, planning tax strategies, spotting legal problems and representing the estate in court if necessary. Schedules of assets, tax returns, notices and miscellaneous documents are prepared by paralegals and secretaries. As a result, probate costs on the whole are probably less than under the old fee schedule system. Contributing to this, is the fact that many states have greatly modified their probate laws by utilizing different and less formal procedures for modest and less complicated estates. If your state has adopted all or part of the Uniform Probate Code, as many have, there may be available an "informal" process in which there are no court appearances or court supervision—a kind of "do it yourself" process (but best done with the assistance of a knowledgeable attorney).

There may also be fees due the personal representative, customarily payable according to a preset schedule when it's a financial institution. When the personal representative is a surviving spouse, child, or relative, there's often no fee. If money is paid out, it will be taxable to the recipient as ordinary income at a rate generally higher than that of the estate tax. A professional personal representative, such as a bank or a trust company, will always charge a fee.

The trend in the legal profession has been away from the percentage fee. This is fair to both the lawyer and the client. It isn't necessarily the value of the estate that makes for a more involved probate, although usually there is a definite relationship between size and complexity.

The fees for large estates or those representing extraordinary problems and/or substantial assets in real estate or a business may be negotiated either by the decedent during his or her lifetime or by the decedent's personal representative after death.

Services rendered by the lawyer usually include preparation of estate and income tax returns, processing documents relating to joint tenancy etc.

Sometimes, allowing the property to go through probate can reduce estate and inheritance taxes. Such savings can be accomplished by establishing trusts in a will that become effective after death. This approach can (1) avoid part of the taxes that ordinarily would be due when the beneficiary of a trust dies, and (2) eliminate a second probate at the death of the survivor (see Chapter 6).

Generally the cost of processing nonprobate assets (those not owned in the decedent's sole name) is less than that of the probate process. Again, this depends on the complexity of the situation.

Some people like the ease of control and simplicity of sole-name ownership even though this will subject the assets to probate. A blanket statement that probate is always to be avoided is simply untrue. The decision to avoid probate should be made only after a careful review of a person's assets and intentions. There are occasions when probate should be avoided and other times when it should be sought. Before taking any action, consult your attorney. And never be fearful of the probate process.

A WILL IS NOT ENOUGH

Making the transition from wife to widow is difficult, but preliminary planning can render the process easier and avoid many future problems. Here are some steps a husband can take to ease the strain of his death:

Keep vital papers in a convenient place. Arrange a handy depository, such as a safe-deposit box, for insurance policies, deeds, securities, contracts, and notes. This will save time and concern in looking for these documents when they are needed.

The original of your will should be in a safe deposit box or with your personal representative if it is a bank.*

Make certain that adequate liquid assets are available. There should be ready cash and easily converted assets for payments of debts, taxes, and living expenses of the survivors. These can be in the form of life insurance, negotiable securities, or cash in a separate bank or savings account. If there are not sufficient liquid assets, it will be necessary to sell some property, probably at an unfavorable price and possibly incurring additional taxes.

Have an attorney who is familiar with your estate, your will, and your family needs. It's also a good idea to make informal arrangements about the anticipated legal fees.

Write general instructions, describing how you would like personal effects, such as clothes, jewelry, and mementos, disposed of. Do not clutter your will with such specifics. Then attach this infor-

---

*If a bank or trust company is named in the will as Personal Representative, i.e., Executor, it will usually provide storage for the original free of charge.

mal note to your will. Some states have laws that give legal significance to such instructions, and even in states that don't, usually your wishes will be respected by your personal representative.

Treat your spouse as a partner in family financial affairs. Keep your spouse informed about investments, company benefit plans, pension programs, insurance, and other estate plans.

Review your will periodically. A will should be checked periodically to make sure that the provisions conform with changing federal and state laws and your own resources and wishes. Since he will be familiar with your needs, try to schedule this review with the same lawyer who drew your will if you are satisfied with his ability as an estate planner.

GUARDIANSHIP/CONSERVATORSHIP

In addition to supervising the administration of decedents' estates, probate courts supervise the administration of the estates of minors and persons who lack the capacity to handle their own affairs. This category of responsibilities is known as guardianship or conservatorship. It is a fact that as people grow older, their ability to administer business affairs and investments diminishes. In some cases, the decrease is so severe that the individual is unable to handle routine matters, such as banking and record-keeping. In many of these cases, it is necessary to request the court to appoint a suitable guardian or conservator to assist the incapacitated individual. The guardian or conservator must prepare an inventory and file it with the court. Often, a bond is also required to assure the guardian's performance. Periodically, usually annually, he must show all receipts and disbursements for that period. At the death of the incapacitated person, a final account is prepared and submitted to the court. Upon the court's approval, the guardian or conservator is discharged and the assets turned over to the personal representative of the decedent.

The difference between a guardianship and a conservatorship is that in a conservatorship there is no determination of incompetency. We all know of people who are not incompetent but who still need help in handling their affairs—protection from artful and deceitful persons who might take advantage of their lack of ability to handle their own affairs. In both guardianship and conservatorship, there is total involvement by the probate court in the administration of the subject's affairs.

POWER OF ATTORNEY

The law of guardianship must contemplate a wide range of skills and quality of judgment among those appointed guardian. Hence, these laws are necessarily restrictive, requiring court approval before investments can be made, for example. Also, the ward's business affairs are exposed to public scrutiny, since all matters related to the guardianship must be filed with the court.

Families who find themselves in these circumstances sometimes try to avoid guardianship through means which often are not effective or satisfactory. For example, occasionally an elderly person will grant a power of attorney to a spouse, child, or friend. Although some states have passed laws allowing these powers to remain in force after the person granting them has become mentally incompetent (durable powers of attorney), the basic rule is that such powers terminate upon the death or incapacity of the person giving them. In any event, often banks and others in the financial community are reluctant to conduct substantial transactions on the basis of powers of attorney. Durable powers of attorney should be granted only to a person who is most trusted. For more on the durable power of attorney see page 34.

Sometimes a person will add a trusted party, such as a child or a friend, as a cosigner or joint tenant on bank accounts. The purpose is to allow the cosigner to make withdrawals and expenditures for the benefit of the owner of the account. Unfortunately, at the death of the owner, the cosigner usually receives the balance of the account by operation of law, which may not have been the intention of the owner and, in fact, may conflict with his general estate plan.

In some circumstances, usually involving modest estates, guardianship or conservatorship may be the only solution. But in cases where estates are more substantial, the creation of an inter vivos trust is much better if competency is not a problem. Here the transition of administration from owner to trust can be smooth, private, and without the expenses of a bond and the restrictions of guardianship law.

4

The truth about joint tenancy

Many people believe that the use of joint tenancy is always the wisest course. They like dual ownership because it allows them to manage their assets and because of the relative ease with which property can be transferred at death. Joint tenancy can accomplish a lot of good, but it's like a doctor's prescription: It should be taken in the proper dosage.

After years of experience in estate planning and settlement, we believe that there is no pat formula that can be applied to all situations. Joint ownership can be useful, but it can also cause difficulties. Questions can arise regarding control of assets during life and taxes after death. Often, the problems do not occur until many years after the original registration, usually when one of the joint tenants has died.

Always consult a lawyer before you decide on joint ownership of anything, be it a home, a condominium, commercial real estate, securities, savings, or even a checking account.

In estate planning, most husbands and wives have similar goals. They want to be sure that in case of death, the survivor will be well provided for, and that when the survivor dies, what is left will go, quickly and easily, to the children.

Joint tenancy may be the wise course in specific situations, but each decision regarding ownership should be made on the basis of a review of the total picture: all your assets, your family circumstances, your overall estate plan, and tax considerations.

If you asked a bank or a savings and loan association how best to set up a $10,000 inheritance, chances are that you would be advised to establish the account in joint tenancy between you and your spouse. It would probably be explained to you that if you died, your spouse would get the money automatically, without the necessity of probate. This could be wise counsel; it would depend on the nature and extent of your other assets and on your estate planning intentions.

One thing is sure: If the advice is good advice, it was by accident. The officer in charge of savings accounts would never be so presumptuous as to inquire into your other assets, your family's financial background and needs, or your own plan for your estate after death—all the data necessary for sound advice. His responsibility is limited to advising you on the various plans offered by his institution.

In our experience, joint tenancy is suitable for the household checking account, small savings accounts, and title to your home. It provides:

A sense of family security. It's a partnership that gives a feeling of greater group security, unity, and harmony than it is possible to get with individual ownership.

Convenience. Bank accounts in joint tenancy can be easily liquidated or drawn upon, by either co-owner, for emergency needs.

Protection of property from claims after death. In many states, certain jointly owned property is not subject to claims made by creditors of the deceased co-owner.

This exemption can also apply to damage/injury claims. If one joint tenant dies as the result of an automobile accident in which he was at fault, and the insurance coverage was inadequate, a judgment exceeding the insurance policy limit could not be collected against assets held in joint tenancy.

Avoidance of publicity. Prompt transfer of ownership can be completed without the publicity that may accompany the probate of a will.

Reduction of estate administration costs. Since ownership of joint tenancy property passes automatically to the co-owner at the death of the other partner, adminstration expenses are not applicable to that part of the estate when probated under a will. This eliminates a lot of legal hocus-pocus and can mean lower settlement bills.

DISADVANTAGES OF JOINT TENANCY

Some of the negative aspects of joint tenancy include:

Loss of control. In most cases, joint tenancy reduces a person's legal control over property. If you have a joint bank account and become ill, the other joint tenant can withdraw sums of money against that account without your knowledge or consent. You may wake up one morning to find that your spouse has withdrawn all of your money and left town—and there's nothing you can do about it!

Need for complete agreement. Decisions on how jointly held property is to be used, managed, and invested must be made harmoniously. Such unanimity can be difficult to achieve if there's a divorce (dissolution), separation, or intrafamily dispute. For example:

- At the time of property settlement discussions in the event of the divorce, your spouse may demand your share of the joint tenancy on the grounds that the other half already belongs to your spouse and should not be involved in the negotiations.
- You and your son own your home together. You both agree to sell, but your son's wife says no. Under some circumstances, she may be able to stop the transaction because of her interest in her husband's real estate.
- You and your daughter jointly own stock. You want to sell, but she refuses to sign the certificates. There's no way to complete the sale without resorting to legal action.

Loss of right to dispose of property at death. A person who places property in joint ownership usually gives up the right to dispose of it in his will. This is so even though you state in your last testament that all your property is to go to someone other than the co-owner.

You may have set up the joint tenancy as a matter of convenience while you were incapacitated, but with no intention that the surviving joint tenant should receive all your property at your death. However, if you die while in the hospital, the other owner may very well get every dime in that joint account, and a legal fight is almost sure to follow.

What it comes down to is that you can have the fanciest will in town, but if everything you own is set up in joint tenancy, in all probability the will isn't worth the paper it's written on, since joint tenancy usually takes precedence. As already pointed out, if you leave your assets in joint ownership and simultaneously dispose of them in some other way in your will, there may be a court battle.

The fact that property is in joint tenancy does not mean that legal procedures can be competely avoided when one of the joint tenants dies. The title to the property will have to be cleared. The name of the person who has died must be removed from the title. This often requires the filing of affidavits and death certificates, and sometimes obtaining tax clearance.

There are some tax considerations related to joint tenancy. Usually income from jointly held property is taxable to each joint owner in proportion to ownership. This may have some significance to husbands and wives who live in states which do not provide for a joint tax return in the manner of the federal government. Under the Economic Recovery Tax Act of 1981, at the death of one joint tenant where the joint tenant's are spouses, one half of the value of the property for federal estate tax purposes will be included in the estate of the deceased joint tenant.

Example: George Smith and his wife, Mary, own a real estate investment, an apartment house in joint tenancy. George dies and at the time of his death the apartment house has a value of $300,000. Only $150,000 of value will be included in George's estate for federal estate tax purposes. This is different from pre-1982 federal law where possibly all of the value may have been included in George's estate. It is important to note that under the new law only George's half will receive a new stepped up tax basis. Mary's half will carry the old pre-death tax basis. If the Smiths had paid $100,000 for the apartment, George's half will have a stepped up basis of $150,000 while Mary's half will retain its old basis of $50,000. A sale of the property for $300,000 after George's death will cause a capital gains tax on Mary's half of the difference between her $50,000 basis and $150,000.

Where the joint tenants are not married to one another, their joint tenancy property is presumed to have been owned *entirely* by the first joint tenant who dies; not half, but all. This presumption can be overcome only by proof that the property or some portion of it was paid for by the survivor from his own funds or that it was placed in joint tenancy solely for convenience, e.g. to allow dual access to funds.

Possible gift taxes. There is no federal gift tax when spouses create or terminate joint tenancies after 1981.

Establishing joint tenancy between nonspouses, on the other hand, can subject the transaction to gift taxes. If you purchase securities or real estate and then place title in joint ownership with someone other than your spouse, you may have to pay a gift tax on one half of the value of the property. Under IRS interpretation, the gift tax takes effect when one person becomes entitled to more than he or she put in.

There can also be trouble in the future if you decide to sever the joint ownership. You may then get hit with another gift tax, this time on the half of the property you previously gave away. It all depends.

There is one important exception to jointly held property subject to gift taxes: stocks in street-name brokerage accounts (held by the broker). If either joint owner can deal with the account alone and make withdrawals without the consent of the other, no gift tax is imposed until the noncontributor withdraws completely.

Under all circumstances, when you are considering entering into or withdrawing from joint tenancy, consult a lawyer to make sure you do not run afoul of tax laws.

LIMITED USE OF JOINT TENANCY. When the total value of property is modest (say a $10,000 bank account or a $75,000 home), there is probably no reason why both should not be held in joint tenancy. If anything happens to either spouse, the survivor will need the money and the house.

With substantial estates—say, a net worth, including life insurance death proceeds, of over $600,000—joint tenancy with a spouse generally should be limited to the homestead and household checking accounts. There should be a will which establishes a trust and provides for an alternate distribution if the spouse dies shortly thereafter or in a common disaster.

In most cases, a homemaker has done a good job handling income, but she has not had much experience with principal. Now, all of a sudden, when circumstances and grief may cloud her ability to reason clearly, she must manage a lot of money. She has almost complete freedom to do with it whatever she wishes.

In many cases a homemaker may be inexperienced, and usually she will be under pressure from relatives anxious to share her grief (and the assets). They think they want to protect the assets from unscrupulous promoters, and from well-meaning but often impractical friends. Her brother may urge her to buy shares in a South American get-rich-quick scheme or, with a little encouragement from her neighbors, she may decide to fulfill her dreams and splurge with a remodeled kitchen, a new vacation home, or an around-the-world trip.

There's nothing wrong with a widow using some of her assets for any legitimate expenditure, as long as she realizes her financial limitations and fulfills her responsibilities to the children. Many women do a better job of managing money than their husbands did. But almost everyone can benefit from the counsel and cautionary advice of a competent trustee named in a will or provided through an agreement entered into during the husband's lifetime.

Joint tenancy and estate tax savings. The time to avoid estate taxes is *before* death. Too many people delay, or refuse to take, protective steps such as providing a trust either during their lifetime or to become effective at death. Once a person has received property outright, as a surviving joint tenant, the only way by which estate taxes can then be reduced is by making gifts, which, in turn, may be subject to costly taxes.

If a man has a $1,000,000 estate, he could establish trusts that would make certain that his widow, while she lives, would have the economic benefit from his property, and, at her death, she would be able to pass all of the principal on to her children without any federal estate tax being imposed at either the husband's death or the subsequent demise of the wife.*

By employing refinements of this trust technique, the Rockefellers, Kennedys, and other wealthy families have been successful in avoiding debilitating taxes for generations. However, the 1976 Tax Reform Act now taxes "generation-skipping" trusts.

You may say, "Yes, that's O.K. for the very rich, but I'm not in that league." In many cases, this is not true: You may be in that league and not know it!

Wealthy people may be able to save more dollars on taxes than you can, but they are also in a better position to pay them. People with modest estates who save a few thousand tax dollars benefit far more percentagewise than do their rich counterparts. Sit down with your lawyer or tax adviser and see for yourself. For tax reasons alone, look hard at joint tenancy and make certain that the savings in probate expenses are not outweighed by unnecessary taxes.

No substitute for a will. Many people think that one of the big advantages of joint ownership is that it eliminates the bother and expense of making a will. This is partially true at times, but more often, it can be faulty—and costly—reasoning.

ARE THERE ANY ALTERNATIVES?

Durable power of attorney. Your mother is getting on in years. Your father died some years ago. Mom has about $100,000 in savings accounts and certificates of deposit, primarily from the sale of the homestead. It was getting to be too much for her. She now lives in an apartment, but because of the infirmities of advancing years, she is fearful of having to go into a medical care facility and if something like that does happen to her, she wants to make sure her funds are properly handled. She has three children and she wants her estate to go to them equally. A good friend of hers has just given her some

---

*After 1986, $600,000 will pass without tax. This is in addition to the unlimited marital deduction that became available to married persons in 1982.

advice. The friend said that she should put all her assets into joint tenancy with her daughter, the one who lives the closest to her and is the most attentive to her, so that the daughter can handle her affairs and spend the money for her during her lifetime. Your mother just received some bad advice—well meaning but, all the same, bad advice.

What should she do? She should keep her assets in her own name, have a will prepared for her that leaves her estate equally to her three children, and give the attentive daughter a durable power of attorney.

All states have laws that in effect provide that one person may give another person a power of attorney to act in his place. All that is necessary is that the person be competent at the time he or she is giving the power of attorney. Until recently, many states had laws that provided that when a person became incompetent, the power of attorney previously granted was no longer valid.

A number of states have adopted what is called a durable power of attorney. The word "durable" means that all that is necessary is that the person granting the power be competent at the time of the grant, and should the person later on become incompetent, the power of attorney continues in existence.

It can be seen that a durable power of attorney is exactly "what the doctor ordered" for older persons. It can serve as a guardianship or conservatorship substitute as well as a good alternative to joint tenancy.

Powers of attorney can be very restrictive or very broad. Usually, when a durable power of attorney is granted it is a broad power of attorney. This means that the person acting under the power of attorney will have the broadest authority to handle the affairs of the person making the grant.

One word of caution. Because most durable powers of attorney are broad, they should only be granted to someone you thoroughly trust.

Totten trust. Assume a husband and wife who have both worked have accumulated savings of $200,000. Rather than put their savings in joint tenancy, it might be prudent for them to take savings and each set up a Totten trust for the other.

THE TRUTH ABOUT JOINT TENANCY

A Totten trust is nothing more than a "payable on death" bank account. The bank account will usually read "John Doe in trust for Mary Doe." It means that if John Doe dies, the bank account belongs to Mary Doe. Mary Doe would take her separate funds and set them up as "Mary Doe in trust for John Doe," and then if Mary Doe dies, they will pass to John Doe. Everything is kept separate. The beneficiary has no right to the funds in the account of the other until the death of the person who established it. Savings accounts, saving certificates, and most mutual funds can be registered in this manner.

We repeat: Before you consider joint tenancy for any property, consult a lawyer and make your decision on the basis of your total present and projected assets, your family circumstances and needs, and your overall estate planning. And do it *now*.

5

Trusts

| A TRUST CAN | Manage property for you and your family
Extend beyond your lifetime
Keep your financial affairs private
Save taxes |

In the legal agreement known as a trust, assets are turned over to someone else to hold and manage for the benefit of yourself and/or others. Trusts, in varying forms, can be used to avoid or postpone taxes, to preserve the privacy of an individual's estate, and to provide a means of controlling or administering property for yourself and/or for others.

The first trusts were created centuries ago in England to disguise the actual ownership of property in order to circumvent feudal obligations and laws. A man would convey real estate to another person under a private arrangement which provided that the benefits from the property would flow to the creator of the trust or others while the legal ownership was held by the trustee.

The trust agreement is a written document that details the manner in which the trustee is to hold the property, the purpose for which its income and principle are to be used, and the duration of the arrangement. In a sense, the trustee is a kind of manager responsible for the care and maintenance of the property, collection of income, and conduct of all business associated with the property; finally, and most importantly, the trustee must account for the administration of the trust to the trustor and/or beneficiaries. The trustee is a fiduciary. The trustee owes a high degree of responsibility to the one creating the trust and to the beneficiaries of the trust.

Some trusts can be established by filling out a printed form, but it is always best to have the agreement prepared by a lawyer experienced in estate planning and probate. There are technical details relating to ownership, taxes, and control of the property that an attorney will be better equipped to deal with than a layman. Some states have laws that limit the trustee's powers and rights and set ranges for fees.

The trustee is paid from the income or assets of the trust, but if he so desires, he can waive compensation. To be safe, have your attorney spell out exactly what the trustee can and cannot do. And to be doubly safe, designate a successor trustee who would be able to take over in case of the first trustee's resignation, death, or disability.

There are no rules limiting the size of a trust. A trust can be for a sum as small as $10,000 or as large as $100 million. Because of the expense of preparation and maintenance, there are, of course, practical minimums. A simple trust can be set up in a short time for a modest fee. More complicated agreements, involving huge sums or special conditions, can require weeks of work and thus be expensive in dollars. But usually these costs will not be significant in relation to the assets in the trust.

State laws vary in detail, but the same broad principles apply. *The measure of a worthwhile trust is its purpose, not the cost of drawing it or the assets involved.*

ADVANTAGES OF A TRUST

It delays and controls distribution of property after death. The trust affords a means of avoiding the problems that arise when beneficiaries are not in a position to handle their inheritance at the time of the donor's demise. The management of property requires judgments regarding investments, expenditures of income and principal, tax planning, accounting, and safekeeping. Not all beneficiaries are able to perform these functions. The trust can provide as little or as much as the creator of the trust thinks wise.

If a man has a will drawn to provide for outright distribution to his heirs, his estate will be allocated according to its terms. The distribution is made after all claims, taxes, and other expenses have been paid. Whether this takes place in a few months or several years depends on the complexity of the estate and the tax problems, if any. The age of the heirs is always a significant factor.

Example: Mr. Baxter's beneficiaries are his seventy-five-year-old mother, who is in poor health, his sixteen-year-old son, still unable to handle money well, and his eight-year-old daughter.

A simple will might provide that each of the beneficiaries receive an outright inheritance upon completion of the probate process. But then the problems begin.

The elderly woman may not be able to care for herself, much less her share of the estate, possibly resulting in the worsening of her health and adversely affecting the value of the inheritance. If she is judged legally incompetent, the court will have to appoint a guardian before that share of the property can be sold or mortgaged or its income reinvested.

The inheritance of the son will usually be held in guardianship until he comes of legal age. In many states, majority is now attained at age eighteen, ready or not!

The young daughter will have to have a guardian named to care for her and her property. And even if she is unable to manage her assets when she is legally an adult, the guardianship will probably terminate.

Guardianships rarely last beyond minority, except when an individual is mentally incompetent or completely dependent.

Trusts can solve all these problems. They can provide for responsible administration and management until the death of the grandmother and until the children are able to take control. Under the trust agreement, each beneficiary would receive all the funds available for support and/or education.

A trust is valuable when it comes to children because it assures that they will receive the benefits of the estate without giving them control. If you have qualms about a youngster's management ability, you can arrange for the trustee to be responsible until the child reaches whatever age you set.

This raises a perplexing question: What is the proper age for children to receive an inheritance? The answer to that question will depend on the individuals involved, but here are some guidelines:

Legally, the child becomes an adult at eighteen, nineteen, or twenty-one, according to the law of the state of residence. If the trust entails large sums, it may be that the young person may be forced to accept more responsibility than he or she can handle. For example, your son may have done a good job handling small sums but have no experience in investment or money management. Furthermore, he may be at an age when personal pressures weigh him down. Perhaps he is completing his college education and making a career choice, or planning marriage or postgraduate training. His decision may mean geographic relocation to an area where he will not be able to consult relatives or family friends.

One solution that can be good for almost everyone is to arrange for an installment distribution of the trust: perhaps 10 percent now, 50 percent when the beneficiary is twenty-five years of age, and so on. This arrangement provides a reasonable method of passing on your estate, minimizes the likelihood of frivolous waste, and makes it possible for the estate assets to continue to grow.

Such a course of action may seem callous and arbitrary, but you must remember that you worked hard to acquire your property and so want it to be put to the best possible use.

We have seen cases in which giving full control of substantial sums to a young person did more harm than good. The use of a partial payment raises the question of whether your children, when they receive a portion of your property at a set age, will waste the assets and, when they receive the next portion, do so again. It is to be hoped that they will learn by experience and be able to handle future installments with more skill and better judgment.

There are other possible arrangements. You can (1) plan for payments from the trust to be related to the needs of the recipient: for example, the beneficiary will receive more money at the start of his career, when earnings are low; or (2) set up a trust whereby the beneficiary receives all income but is not permitted to touch the principal. If the estate is large, this plan can have considerable merit.

In each case, what you decide to do should depend on the individual beneficiary and the assets involved. The beauty of the trust is that you get to write your own family financial plan.

With an income-only trust, you may create psychological problems by overprotecting the beneficiary. The heir may become dependent on the trust income and thus, ultimately, be harmed rather than aided. One of the factors motivating us to work, to create, and to provide for ourselves and our families is the uncertainty of tomorrow. Eliminate this uncertainty and you remove a valuable psychological prod. It may be true that most people continue to work after receiving an inheritance, but the impact of a large sum of money should be considered before the trust papers are completed.

From our experience, we do not believe that the distribution of any estate to a young person should be delayed beyond the thirty-fifth birthday except in special circumstances, as with a severely handicapped child or in a case involving such large sums that estate tax savings may make delay the most economical means of conserving wealth from one generation to the next. If the person is unable to handle an inheritance at the age of thirty-five, the chances are that he never will.

It avoids probate and guardianship. Through the device of a guardianship, a legal parent is provided for an individual who is incapable of managing his affairs because he is too young or lacks the requisite mental capacity. Usually, a guardian is appointed by the probate court in the county in which the ward (the individual being cared for) lives.

There are two types of guardianship:

1. *Guardian of the person.* A guardian of the person concerns himself with the ward's housing, food, clothing, medical bills, schooling, and other necessities. This type of guardian is usually a relative or family friend who knows the child and, presumably, has the ward's love and respect.
2. *Guardian of the estate.* This expression refers to an individual or a corporation, such as a bank, appointed to control and manage the ward's estate and property for the benefit of the ward. When the guardian is not a professional, the court may require the purchase of a bond to cover faithful performance. By means of such an insurance agreement, a guarantee is obtained against any possible financial loss caused by the default of the guardian. The court retains jurisdiction over administration, receives annual reports of actions and expenditures, and in some cases, must approve large distributions or decisions involving significant outlays.

The costs of providing for the guardianship of an estate can be high. The annual cost of a fidelity bond can be as much as one half of one percent of the value of the property being administered, and usually there will also be legal and guardian fees.

Guardianships of minors terminate when the legal age is attained. In many states this means eighteen, which most would agree is not the best time to take on the responsibility of a substantial inheritance.

Generally, the same person assumes both guardianship roles. With large estates, however, it may be wise to divide the responsibilities.

A trust can eliminate the need for the guardian of the estate since property in trust is not subject to the probate process. It is set up for the heirs and distributed by the trustee in accordance with the terms of the trust agreement.

It provides a flexible means of administration and accomodation to change. The primary objective of estate planning, especially as concerns preparation of wills, is to prepare for problems that may occur one day. Here are typical questions we have encountered from clients:

- How much of his inheritance should my son spend for care and support?
- Should the trustee give him money to buy a new automobile or power boat?
- Should an artistically gifted daughter have funds to study abroad? And if she marries, how can I be sure that her funds from me will not be used improvidently by her husband?
- Should arrangements be made to provide my son with money with which to start a business or profession?
- How should the costs of postgraduate education be handled?
- What if my daughter wants to delay a career choice by attending graduate school?

It's hard to answer such queries as these correctly at any time, but it is even more difficult to do so before the situations arise, when you are making out your will. These decisions are important because, by law, after your death your last wishes must be carried out by your executor exactly as the terms of your will provide, no matter how conditions may have changed between then and the time of your signature.

Here again, the best answer, for many people asking such questions, is to create a trust. This arrangement transfers the decision-making power to a trustee and thus delays the need for a detailed solution until the problem arises.

The flexibility of the trust allows the trustee to make choices on the basis of the situation at the time, yet still work within the broad guidelines set forth in the trust agreement.

This ability to change is especially important with investments. Trustees need to be able to shift securities that will produce the best results for the trust. In the past, many trusts restricted investments—to railroad bonds in the 1920s and to anything but real estate and common stocks in the late 1930s as the result of Depression bankruptcies. Such restrictions hampered trustees, resulting in decreased financial returns and lower appreciation, because following World War II there was a meteoric rise in common stocks that provided considerable protection against the erosion of inflation. In creating a trust, therefore, the best rule is to provide flexible investment powers and let the trustee adapt to take advantage of the best and safest opportunities.

It provides professional managers and advisers. There are three ways to get professional management when creating a trust: directly, by appointing a bank or trust company as trustee; indirectly, by empowering an individual trustee to retain advisers; or by a combination of both methods.

Many people typically say when thinking of arranging for a trustee: "I want somebody with a heart—somebody who will take care of my family." They fear that the professional will be impersonal and cold-hearted, that a trust officer will not be able to give the widow and children the sympathy and understanding they want and may need.

Although such fears are sometimes justified, we have found, through long experience, that usually the mark of a competent trust officer is his ability to help beneficiaries. Most of the men and women holding the position of trustee enjoy their work and become genuinely concerned with the personal problems of the beneficiaries. There is, of course, a limit to the time and effort they can give. If you feel that it is important for the trustee to have a personal involvement with your family, consider naming a cotrustee—perhaps your spouse, son, sister-in-law, or cousin—to work with the professional.

It saves on taxes. This advantage is explained in detail later, but broadly speaking, trusts can reduce or even eliminate taxes by:

1. *Dividing income among beneficiaries.* Income taxes are computed on a graduated scale: the more income, the higher the tax rate. By spreading the available income among two or more taxpayers, the tax is often lessened. In other words, "sprinkling" lowers the tax bracket and, thus, the tax.
2. *Withholding ownership rights.* A trust may be created so that the beneficiary, say a spouse, is not considered the "owner" of the property in the trust. The beneficiary may receive all income and even some part of the principal if she needs it to maintain her standard of living. At her death, the property will not be taxed because, in tax and trust law terms, she is not considered the "owner." This is one of the most important features of a properly drawn trust and is responsible for millions of dollars of estate tax savings every year. More will be said about this particular feature of trusts in Chapter 6.
3. *Transferring income tax burdens.* Trusts can shift the obligation to pay taxes on property income from a high tax bracket person to a person or persons in lower tax brackets. This can be done on a permanent basis with a gift in trust or on a temporary basis with a "short-term" trust.

TYPES OF TRUSTS

Each of the many possible types of trusts can be described in terms of its suitability for a specific situation. Keep in mind that a trust is affected by tax codes and other laws which are complex, and therefore it should be drawn by an experienced attorney after careful consideration of the possible contingencies. In broad terms, trusts can be categorized in the following ways:

Trusts under will (testamentary trusts). According to this most common method of establishing trusts, the will provides that at death, all or a portion of the estate will be administered by a trustee who will make distributions to certain individuals or organizations. Such a trust assures that your wishes will be carried out and that your beneficiaries will be treated properly. Usually, this type of trust also results in tax savings.

Example: Mr. Lewis has an estate of $300,000. His seventy-year-old wife has little knowledge of finance and tends to be a spendthrift. In his will, Mr. Lewis sets up a trust whereby his widow will be assured of $30,000 annually. The trustee bank is directed to pay her $2,500 each month. At a 6 percent annual return, this nest egg will last sixteen years; at 7 percent, eighteen years; at 8 percent, twenty-one years, and so on. If the trust yields an 8 percent return in the first year, the trust will earn $24,000. Therefore, the annual payment of $30,000 will deplete the principal or corpus of the trust by $6,000, and so on. And at 10 percent—not an unusual situation these days—no encroachment on principal will be necessary.

When children are involved, trusts under will can be flexible and set up to meet changing conditions. Typically, a *sprinkling trust* permits the trustee to distribute income and principal according to the specific needs of each of the beneficiaries.

Example: Mr. McCormick has three children: a son finishing dental college, a daughter married to a missionary, and a second son, who has recurrent health problems. The father wants to help each child but recognizes that the financial requirements of each may vary each year. He establishes a sprinkling trust so that the trustee has full power to allocate the $10,000 annual income according to the needs of the children. Here's how such a trust might work:

> Year 1 The oldest son receives $6,000 to help him start his practice. The others get $2,000 each.

Year 2 The daughter, back home from abroad, is building a house, so she gets $5,000 and the balance is split between the two sons.

Year 3 The younger son becomes ill, so he receives $6,000, while $2,000 goes to each of the other children.

This example demonstrates how properly drawn trusts can be flexible and permit the trustee to provide humane as well as financial protection.

Inter vivos trusts. These "among living" trusts enable specific property to be administered and distributed during the lifetime of the creator. They are popular and widely used because: (1) property held in a living trust is not subject to the formalities of probate; (2) professional management can be designated for special investments such as real estate; (3) if it's irrevocable (cannot be terminated), income taxes can be saved by shifting income from the trustor, who is in a high tax bracket, to the beneficiary, who pays taxes at a lower rate; and (4) privacy of family finances can be maintained by avoiding probate.

Life insurance trust. This is like a living trust except that its only assets are insurance policies and, thus, during the trustor's lifetime there is no management responsibility. The trust is merely the beneficiary of the insurance. When the insured dies, the death proceeds will be paid to the trust, not an individual.

Usually, the insured person continues to pay the premiums and the trust lies dormant until he dies. But it is also possible to fund such a trust—to set up assets whose income is used to pay the premiums during the lifetime of the insured.

Most such trusts are revocable. During his lifetime, the insured retains all rights to the insurance and can cancel or borrow against the cash value of the policies. But irrevocable life insurance trusts are also possible and in special situations make sound estate planning sense!

A life insurance trust is useful for young professionals such as physicians, dentists, and lawyers, who, in their early careers, are unable to accumulate large assets directly or through personal retirement and profit-sharing plans. Frequently, they carry substantial life insurance in order to create a sizable estate quickly, thus protecting their young families from the loss of their income-producing ability.

Another advantage is that a life insurance trust will not be subject to probate, so there will be no delays and, except in rare cases, neither the proceeds nor the income will be subject to creditors' claims.

Gifts in trust. This type of trust enables you to give property when you are not sure of the recipient's ability to manage the assets, as with grandchildren or older relatives. It provides a convenient way to help others and also to avoid estate taxes on property that has appreciated between the date of the gift and the donor's death.

With such a trust, there is some measure of control and discretion in the use of the funds because the property is held in trust and administered by a designated trustee for the benefit of the recipient(s).

Gift trusts are often used by older people planning ways to reduce their future tax liabilities and, at the same time, to provide current financial aid to grandchildren for educational expenses, or to a charitable institution for special programs or continuing financial support.

Charitable trusts. Usually, these are family foundations, designed to make gifts to charitable institutions for the purpose of creating a memorial for the donors, their loved ones, or their families. In many cases, the trusts are set up when the wealthy individual is dissatisfied with the methods by which the charities administer or distribute funds or discovers a particular charitable cause that is unfunded.

Once they are established, they must be maintained, must make annual contributions, and must file voluminous reports—so it's not advisable to consider creating such funds unless substantial sums are involved.

The concept of charitable gifts is excellent and praiseworthy. Moreover, under present tax laws, gifts to charitable institutions which meet IRS qualifications are income tax deductible. But before you take action, make sure that the recipient agency is well run and will use your gift wisely.

If you want to make a sizable donation to a hospital, university, or social agency, check the capabilities and management of the potential recipient and consult an experienced attorney. In most cases, you will find that the charitable organization has the resources, background, and personnel to handle money more effectively than a trustee who is inexperienced in this specialized area.

From the charity's viewpoint, cash is usually most welcome, but for the donor, this seldom provides the greatest tax benefits. Usually, it is most advantageous to give property which has appreciated in value. The cost will be low and the tax deduction will be based on the current market value.

On the other hand, such gifts—often real estate or shares of a closely held corporation—tend to be illiquid. Once they become the property of the institution, they can be sold without the approval or knowledge of the donor.

Charitable remainder trust. This is an arrangement which will give you an immediate income tax deduction for your charitable contribution, will help to lower your estate taxes, and can provide income for you while the property is in trust. You establish a trust and arrange for the charity to get the money or property at some future date, usually at your death.

The amount you can deduct is based on IRS tables which consider your age, the value of the property, and the income from the trust. Generally, the older you are when you set up such a trust, the greater your deduction will be. But the IRS limits the deductions for gifts to public charities to 50 percent of your adjusted gross income when the gift is cash; to 30 percent (in most cases) when the donation involves appreciated securities. If the annual deductions exceed these limits, you can carry forward the excess for five years. A charitable remainder trust can also be established at your death for the benefit of another person—say your spouse—with the remainder of the trust to go to charity at the beneficiary's death.

These trusts require precise drafting, so always consult a tax-wise attorney. And make certain that the recipient is an organization for which gifts are deductible under IRS standards.

Revocable and irrevocable trusts. All trusts fall into one or the other of these categories, each of which has its advantages and disadvantages.

A person establishing a revocable trust retains the right to revoke it at any time. This type of trust may be used when the trustor is not sure how well the trust will be administered or how long he may want it to exist.

Example: Dr. Grass, a widower, has accumulated $500,000. He wants to leave his estate to his children, some of whom are still minors, but he is not convinced that a professional trustee will make the most rewarding investments or provide the personal empathy that he feels his children will need. Therefore, he establishes a revocable trust and names a bank as trustee.

After two years, he decides that the bank does not suit his wishes and revokes the trust. If Dr. Grass should die while the trust is in effect, these assets will be included in his taxable estate and thus subject to taxation.

With a revocable trust, you can keep adding to the assets as long as you live. Or if you suffer financial reverses, you can withdraw some assets from it.

An irrevocable trust is the opposite. A person establishing this type of trust loses the right to terminate the agreement, cannot receive any income, cannot use the assets as collateral for a loan or in any way exercise control of the trust. If the creator of an irrevocable trust retains any of these types of benefits in the trust assets, the IRS will consider the trust revocable and a part of the creator's taxable estate.

At the death of the one establishing an irrevocable trust, if he retained no rights, the property will not be considered a part of his estate, but the value of the trust at the date of the gift will be included in the estate for purposes of calculating the unified federal tax credit.

Irrevocable trusts have two advantages: (1) the income from the trust assets are not taxable to the trustor; (2) the appreciation, over the years, will not be taken into account for estate tax purposes.

Short-term trusts. Many trusts are structured to pass on property, but short-term trusts are created primarily to avoid income taxes. They transfer income from someone with a high tax rate to someone else, in a much lower tax bracket. In theory, short-term trusts are advantageous; in practice, they are suitable only in a limited number of situations.

By law, a short-term trust has a minimum life of the lesser of ten years or the lifetime of the individual for whose benefit the trust will operate. While the property is in trust, all its income goes to the beneficiary. On termination, the principal reverts to the original donor.

Use short-term trusts cautiously. Remember that you must be ready to accept loss of control over your property for a long time and also be willing to have all its income go to someone else.

In some situations, this kind of arrangement can be dangerous—for example, when the transferred assets are highly specialized, such as real estate, which requires personal attention, or stock representing the controlling interest in a corporation. Once the trust is established, there's nothing the donor can do about it!

Watch the tax angle. All distributed income is taxable to the beneficiary at regular income tax rates. If the beneficiary, often a child or needy relative, receives unexpected income, his tax bracket will be so high that there will no longer be any tax advantage.

Don't get carried away by the idea of tax avoidance. Ten years is a long time during which many changes can take place in your own fortunes and in those of the people you seek to help.

Generally, short-term trusts are suitable for high-income families who, temporarily, can afford to spare some or all of their investment income but want to get back both the capital gains and earning power of the property.

Specifically, short-term trusts are often used for:

Supporting an aged parent. Mr. O'Toole, who is in the 50 percent tax bracket, contributes $3,200 to the support of his eighty-year-old mother. Because of taxes, he has to earn $6,400 to provide this sum.

He has $40,000 in 8 percent bonds that yield $3,200 annually. He uses them to set up a short-term trust that will continue for ten years or as long as his mother lives.

This arrangement assures the needed income, and Mr. O'Toole will pay less in taxes because his reportable income will be lower. At his mother's death, he will get back the $40,000—or more, if the property has appreciated in value.

College trust. Mr. Ross has an eight-year-old daughter who, he expects, will start college in ten years. His taxable income is $50,000, so he's in the 44 percent tax bracket (1982 rate). A short-term trust of $15,000 will provide his daughter with $1,800 a year. There will be no tax on this amount and Mr. Ross will save $792 annually. Mr. Ross will pay the income taxes for his daughter, if any. Through reinvestment of all income and appreciation, the benefits will compound so that when the daughter is eighteen, she will have enough money to pay for most of the tuition costs and, perhaps, some expenses too.*

Minor children. Lawyer Lyon has four children, all under twelve years of age. His net taxable income is $60,000, of which $4,800 represents interest on $60,000 worth of government bonds. He pays a tax of $17,705, so he nets $42,295.

He can save on taxes by setting up four separate trusts, in each of which he places $15,000 in bonds. Each child will then receive $1,200 of income, tax free, and Mr. Lyon gets annual tax savings of $2,112.

As the children grow older and start earning money on their own, they may have to pay taxes, probably at a low 12 percent rate.

Salesman Smith has a twelve-year-old son who wants to be a lawyer and estimates that, at a minimum, the costs of graduate school will be $30,000. In the 44 percent tax bracket, he must tie up $65,000, at a 10 percent annual return, to provide this money.

Mr. Smith sets up a short-term trust with $24,000. At 10 percent, this will compound to the needed sum. Better yet, the father each year will have an extra $1,050 in spendable annual income due to lower taxes.

---

*CAUTION: If funds in a trust are used to satisfy the legal support obligations of the creator of the trust (in some states, this includes college education), the trust will be taxed to the donor.

Gift tax. Establishment of a short-term trust requires that a gift tax return be filed if the value of the income from the trust exceeds the present value of the Donor's annual gift tax exclusion. If a gift tax return has to be filed, then it will mean that some part of the donor's federal unified lifetime credit is used—and most people try to avoid use of any of this credit if possible so that it is available at death. The annual gift tax exclusion, commencing in 1982, was increased from $3,000 per year per Donee to $10,000 per year per Donee. And, if the Donor is married and the Donor's spouse joins in on the gift, the annual exclusion as to any one Donee is increased to $20,000. In practical terms, what this means is that there will be no need to file a gift tax return and use up any lifetime unified credit if both the Donor and the Donor's spouse participate in the establishment of a short-term trust for one Donee and the assets of the trust are worth about $45,000 when the trust is created. If you want to you could do the same thing the following year and bring the total for a particular Donee to $90,000, and if you kept doing it for successive years, an unbelievable amount of wealth could be set aside for a Donee without the Donor encroaching upon the Donor's lifetime credit. Remember, each successive gift must be in a trust for 10 years duration.

Prior to 1982 one of the drawbacks in establishing a short-term trust was the small annual gift tax exclusion. The Donor encroached upon his or her lifetime unified credit (more on this in the next chapter)—and at the end of the ten (10) year period, the Donor received back the assets from the short-term trust and perhaps the Donor received them back at a time when he really didn't need them. We suspect that it may now develop that because of the increased annual gift tax exclusion and because of the method upon which computations are made (the present federal tables use an unrealistically low rate of 6%) there will be an increase in the use of short-term trusts.

These examples show how tax savings can be achieved with short-term trusts. If you feel financially secure enough to get along without substantial funds for ten years, short-term trusts can be useful. But do not place more value on the tax benefits than on personal or family needs.

Interest free loans. As an alternative to a short-term trust, some sophisticated givers are making interest free demand loans to their children or other loved ones. This is done in anticipation that the recipients in turn will invest the funds and the income made on the invested funds will be used by the recipients and taxed to them at their lower income tax rates. This theory of "giving" has thus far stood up in Court, however, the IRS strongly disagrees with it, claiming it really is an assignment of income by the "giver" and the income is taxable to the "giver." Anybody attempting this type of procedure has to be prepared for the possibility that the government will challenge it. If the children you want to give the funds to are not of legal age or even if they are of legal age, and you want to make sure that the principal amount of the loan does not disappear, a trust vehicle should be used. The Trustee holds the principal sum and invests it for the children and the income from the trust investment is taxed to the beneficiary.

REMEMBER Trusts can:
1. Continue beyond your lifetime.
2. Avoid probate.
3. Keep your financial affairs private.
4. Provide professional management.
5. Avoid taxes.
6. Provide a flexible means of administering investments over a period of changing conditions.

6

Estate and inheritance taxes

- **THE VALUE OF A DECEDENT'S PROPERTY IS SUBJECT TO FEDERAL ESTATE TAX LAWS**
- **MOST STATES ALSO LEVY A DEATH TAX**
- **THESE TAXES CAN OFTEN BE SUBSTANTIALLY REDUCED BY THE PROPER USE OF TRUSTS**

In estate planning it is essential to consider the taxes that may be imposed following the death of persons with property. Once you establish your financial objectives and assess your wealth, you need expert assistance to determine how to keep the maximum amount of your estate for your heirs by minimizing inheritance and estate taxes.

The first inheritance tax of the U.S. government was enacted in 1797, but was repealed in 1802. For the next century, the federal estate tax was on and off—revived to help finance wars and repealed with peace. The tax was imposed during the Civil War, repealed in 1870, adopted again in the Spanish-American War, dropped in 1902. In 1916, the federal estate tax as we know it today was established.

Over the years, there have been frequent revisions. There were substantial changes in 1976 and 1978—but by far the most dramatic change took place August 13, 1981. On that date, President Reagan signed into law the *Economic Recovery Act of 1981*. After a 5 year phase-in period, the amount of wealth transferred will have to be at least $600,000 before a federal estate tax will become payable. In addition, starting in 1982, Federal law allows transfers between spouses to be totally exempt from federal gift tax and from federal estate tax. The government decided, just as it does in income tax matters, that married persons should be treated as a unit.

All Wills and other testamentary documents in existence prior to 1982 should be carefully reviewed to make sure full advantage is taken of the new law.

The *Economic Recovery Act of 1981* is almost too good to be true. For instance, it is estimated that if the new law were fully on line in 1981, there would have only been 20,000 federal estate tax returns filed in the entire country, and of those filed only 6,500 would have paid any tax. This would mean that less than ½ of 1% of the persons that died in 1981 would have had to pay any federal estate tax. By way of comparison, the law that was in effect in 1981 required that approximately 111,000 federal estate tax returns be filed and of those filed, 55,000 had to pay a tax.

In addition to the federal estate tax, most states have enacted a death tax, on either the amount a person inherits or on the size of the estate. Some of these levies date back to the early 1800's. The terms *inheritance tax* and *estate tax* have different meanings. An inheritance tax is assessed against the person who receives the property after the death of someone. Normally, this levy is determined by the total amount inherited and the relationship of the beneficiary to the deceased—for example, a son of a decedent would pay taxes at a lower rate than would a cousin of a decedent. An estate tax is imposed on the entire estate and does not necessarily look to the relationship between the heirs and the deceased. Generally, except when the beneficiary is the spouse of the deceased or a charitable beneficiary, the levy is the same no matter who receives the property.

When states have both a state inheritance tax and a state estate tax, the estate tax would be levied only rarely. Usually, the purpose of such a tax is to take advantage of the credit allowed against the federal estate tax for state death taxes where the state inheritance tax is not high enough to use up all the allowable federal credit.

As you add to your assets, review the potential tax liabilities with your attorney and be ready to make changes in your estate plan to reduce taxes and meet requirements of new legislation and regulations.

ESTATE AND INHERITANCE TAXES

Time is an important consideration in the payment of estate and inheritance taxes. The federal tax is due nine months after the date of death, and most states require payment at about the same time or a few months thereafter. However, it is possible to get extensions for both levies. Postponement of payment can be important when the estate is complicated or when substantial property is involved because, to meet tax deadlines, some properties may have to be sold at below-value prices. But watch out for the Federal interest on the tax owed. It is double digit and it is triggered to the prime rate.

For all intents and purposes, all property owned by the decedent at death is subject to tax at its value on the date of death, not on what may have been paid for it when acquired by the decedent. There is no life insurance exemption as far as the federal government is concerned, and when there are state exemptions, they are generally limited to certain amounts, depending on the relationship between the insured and the beneficiary.

The 1981 Federal tax act eased those provisions which allow for the delay in the payment of estate taxes. Under some circumstances, tax payments may be suspended for five years after death and then paid over the succeeding ten-year period. The rate of interest in such cases is also quite favorable.

In all cases concerning death taxes, consult your lawyer. The federal estate tax return is a many paged document available without charge from the U.S. Treasury Department. The new changes in the law that became effective in 1982, are so new that regulations and interpretations have not yet been issued by the Government. Tax experts and the IRS are studying the implications and provisions of the new law. The IRS has not even completed issuing all of its regulations as a result of the 1976 and 1978 changes, so it can be expected that it will take quite some time for all of the interpretations and regulations of the 1981 act to be issued. In addition, as with any substantial tax law, it is to be anticipated that there will be follow-up technical corrections to the 1981 act to straighten out certain drafting mistakes and oversights.

At the present time, these are the highlights of the federal law on the taxation of estates.

1. If the deceased was survived by a spouse, the estate is allowed a further deduction, called the "marital deduction," and for the first time in the history of the federal estate tax law, this marital deduction has become unlimited *IF* the governing instruments are properly drafted so that the assets received by the surviving spouse qualify for the marital deduction. In nearly all instances, it will be to the advantage of the taxpayer to utilize the unlimited marital deduction and thereby postpone the federal estate tax until the death of the surviving spouse.

    To qualify for this important saving, the surviving spouse must be given certain minimum rights to the property, to-wit: the right to all of the income to the total exclusion of anyone else. Property given outright or in joint tenancy qualifies. Prior to 1981, trust arrangements had to provide the surviving spouse with all the income, plus the power at the death of the surviving spouse to dispose of the trust to whomever he or she wanted. In 1982, it is no longer necessary to give the surviving spouse this power. The first of the spouses to die can provide that all of the property set aside in trust for the surviving spouse be set aside in such a manner that the suirviving spouse receives all of the income from it, but on the death of the surviving spouse, it automatically goes to such person(s) or organization(s) as determined by the spouse whose property it was and who was the first to die. This new arrangement is called Qualified Terminable Interest Property.

2. No federal estate tax return need be filed unless the total gross estate (before allowable deductions) is greater than the unified tax credit. The unified credit increases from $64,000 in 1982 to $192,800 in 1987—a six-year phase-in period. This is a credit against the tax, and consequently, there is an exemption equivalent. This is the way it works:

ESTATE AND INHERITANCE TAXES

Year of Death (or gift)	Credit	Exemption Equivalent
1982	$ 64,000	$225,000
1983	77,300	275,000
1984	96,300	325,000
1985	121,800	400,000
1986	155,800	500,000
1987	192,800	600,000

In other words, by 1987, regardless of whether or not a spouse survives, a taxpayer with $600,000 or less in taxable assets will pay no federal estate tax.

These filing requirements assume that no part of any credit (exemption equivalent) is used up by means of gifts made by the decedent after September 8, 1976. See below re: Unification of Estate and Gift Taxes.

3. There's an option to value property at the date of death or within six months from that date. If the estate holds assets which were declining in value at the owner's death, this option allows the estate to avoid some of the sting by permitting the estate tax to be based on the lower value six months after death.

However, the law does state that all assets must be appraised at the same time. You cannot choose different dates for different assets.

4. Deductions from the gross value of the estate are permitted for such expenses as the funeral, administration, debts, mortgages, and liens against the property. What is left after these deductions is the net value, or net estate, which forms the basis for tax calculations.

5. See tables at the end of this chapter for the rates of tax. Although the tables reflect that the rates are from 18% to 65%, in reality the lower rates are not effective because they are offset by the unified credit. The result is that the federal rates actually start, after giving effect to the state death tax credit, in the low 30%'s. The maximum tax rate by 1985 will be 50% for estates over $2,500,000—and after giving effect to

the state credit, the rate drops to as low as 34% on estates in excess of $10,000,000.

UNIFICATION OF ESTATE AND GIFT TAXES

In 1976, an important change was made in the federal taxation of estates. That law unified the estate and gift tax.

At one time gift taxes and estate taxes were separate. There were different schedules for each. This difference was eliminated by the 1976 Federal Tax Reform Act. Today, if you make a gift in excess of the annual gift tax exclusion amount, you eat into your unified tax credit so that when you die there is less unified tax credit available to your estate. An estate tax return does not have to be filed until the gross estate (before allowable deductions) is greater than the remaining unified tax credit of the decedent, a schedule of which is set forth above.

For many years, the annual gift tax exclusion, the amount you could give to any one person without incurring a tax or use of credits or exemptions, was $3,000 per year. Commencing in 1982, the annual exclusion was raised from $3,000 per Donee to $10,000 per Donee.

In addition to the $10,000 per year per Donee gift tax annual exclusion, commencing in 1982, there is an unlimited exclusion for amounts paid directly to an educational institution for tuition and to a health care provider for medical service. There is no restriction on the age of the beneficiary or on the relationship of the beneficiary to the Donor. It is emphasized that to qualify for this unlimited exclusion, the gift must be paid directly to the educational institution or the provider of the medical services and not flow through the Donee.

If both spouses agree, gifts by them to a third party can total $20,000 in any one year to any one Donee without incurring any federal gift tax. However, gift tax returns would have to be filed signifying a spouse's consent.

The federal gift tax return is due on April 15 of the year following the year in which a reportable gift was made. It used to be that gift tax returns had to be filed quarterly. This has been eliminated.

ESTATE AND INHERITANCE TAXES

It is emphasized that the unified tax credit is a lifetime one, so that if, through the years, taxable gifts are made and some of the unified credit is used, only the remainder, if any, is available to reduce the estate tax that might be due when the Donor dies.

It still pays to make gifts of property that are likely to appreciate in value. But generally there are no longer tax incentives for older people to give away assets in excess of the annual exclusion on which substantial appreciation has been achieved. And, with the new $10,000 annual exclusion per Donee, which can increase to $20,000 per Donee if your spouse joins in, a remarkable amount of wealth can be given away in a short period of time.

There no longer is a federal gift tax for transfers between spouses. It is part of the concept of treating married persons as a unit. It is emphasized that this is the federal concept. There are still states that have gift taxes for transfers between spouses.

The giving of property, even between spouses, is something that should be carefully analyzed and our advice is to consult with a knowledgeable lawyer *before* making any substantial gifts. We are living in a world where few things are irrevocable, even long standing marriages. Once property is given away, it cannot be recaptured. Many people like to give property away for what they consider to be tax purposes, and yet hope they can retain a string on it so that if they ever need it it will be returned to them. That is not a gift. If a string is retained you have defeated any tax purpose you might have had in making the gift.

Example: Mr. Jones dies in 1982 with an estate of $400,000 after settlement expenses. No taxable gifts have been made. He leaves everything to his wife. there is no tax because of the unlimited marital deduction. In fact, he could have left $225,000 to someone other than his wife, for instance his children, and there still would not have been a federal estate tax. All he had to make sure of was that the amount over the exemption equivalent was left to his wife in a manner that qualified for the marital deduction. In fact, it may have been prudent in his estate planning to leave $225,000 to his wife in such a way as not to qualify for the marital deduction, but still give her the economic benefits from the $225,000. On her subsequent death, the $225,000 would pass death tax free to whomever he designated. The balance over and above $225,000 would pass to his spouse in such a way as to qualify for the marital deduction and thereby totally avoid the federal death tax but be subject to tax on her subsequent death (at which time her exemption equivalent would be available to her estate).

If Mr. Jones died in 1987, he could leave up to $600,000 to anyone and have no concern as far as federal death taxes are concerned.

In fact, if a husband and wife each own $600,000 in assets, a total of $1,200,000 of their estates can be arranged in such a way that after 1986 the entire $1,200,000 can pass without any federal estate tax. The way it works is that the first spouse to die provides that his or her surviving spouse has all of the assets owned by the first spouse held for him or her in a trust, which purposely does not qualify for the marital deduction, but which provides all of the economic benefits to the surviving spouse. Then, when the surviving spouse dies, those assets automatically pass on to the children, either outright or in a continuing trust arrangement. The first spouse to die utilizes his or her $600,000 exemption equivalent and there is no Federal estate tax. The surviving spouse then likewise provides that his or her $600,000 in assets passes to the other spouse, but because the other spouse has predeceased, then passes to the children, and by utilizing his or her $600,000 exemption equivalent, there is no federal estate tax. The result is $1,200,000 has been passed on to the children free and clear of all federal estate taxes.

It makes sense, in substantial situations, to make sure both spouses have at least $600,000 (by 1987) in their individual estates. This way with properly drafted wills or other testamentary documents, no matter who dies first, full advantage is taken of each spouses lifetime exemption—with the result that a total of $1,200,000 will have passed free and clear of federal death taxes after both spouses have died.

Joint tenancy interests. The federal death tax law that became effective in 1982 provides that all joint tenancies between spouses, regardless of how created will be considered to be owned one-half by each for purposes of the Federal death tax law. In other words, if you

ESTATE AND INHERITANCE TAXES

and your spouse own property totalling $1,000,000 in joint tenancy, it is, for death tax purposes, as though each of you owned $500,000. Joint tenancy property qualifies for the marital deduction so the effect, under federal law, is to totally eliminate any death tax on jointly owned assets when the first spouse dies. The practical effect of spouses holding property in joint tenancy between them is that in the event of the death of one of the joint tenants, the surviving joint tenant will receive a stepped-up basis for income tax purposes on the value of one-half (½) of the property held in joint tenancy, the half that was included in the deceased's joint tenant's estate.

For example, if a married couple own only one piece of property and it is worth $1,000,000, and they paid $50,000 for the property and one of them dies, the survivor will have a basis of $500,000 in one-half (½) of the property and $25,000 in the other one-half (½) of the property.

For the tax treatment of joint tenancy arrangements between persons that are not married to each other, see Chapter 4.

Generation skipping transfers. The law seeks to discourage the establishment of long-term trusts which pass property from generation to generation with little or no estate tax. There is no tax problem when for instance a man leaves property to his wife for life and on her death to their children. But, if instead of giving it outright to the children when the wife dies, it continues to be held in trust for the children and only when they die does it go outright to the grandchildren—you then have a generation-skipping tax potential.

The law does allow an exclusion from the generation-skipping transfer tax of the sum of $250,000 for each child of the decedent who has a child. This sum is a total, regardless of how many grandchildren may be involved. For example: A dies survived by son B, who has three children, and daughter C, who has no children. A's estate would be entitled to a $250,000 generation-skipping transfer exclusion. If C had one or more children, the amount would be $500,000.

There are special provisions which "grandfather in" until January 1, 1983, wills and revocable trusts with generation-skipping features that were in existence on or before June 11, 1976, so be cautious about altering such instruments.

The effect of these new provisions can be avoided somewhat by establishing a series of trusts for each separate generation sometimes called "layered" trusts.

The Federal death tax law has other important aspects, such as special real estate valuation relief for farmers and owners of closely held businesses, and extension of time to pay estate taxes; special rules regarding the taxability of retirement benefits, and many other provisions.

Qualifying for this special relief may prove difficult and many of the new measures may not apply to your personal or family situations. Everyone who has property should retain a knowledgeable attorney to review their estate plan in light of this new law.

CUTTING TAXES ON THE DEATH OF THE SURVIVING SPOUSE

Although the federal death tax may now be eliminated on the death of the first spouse, the idea behind sound tax planning is to reduce the amount of tax otherwise payable on the death of the survivor. Tax-wise attorneys can significantly reduce this tax through the use of a two-trust arrangement.

Example: Mrs. Wilson is left $800,000 outright by her husband who dies in 1987. She will pay no federal estate tax because of the unlimited marital deduction, but, if she doesn't remarry, the federal estate tax on her estate when she dies after giving effect to the state credit will be $65,400.

The estate tax could have been avoided by the creation of two trusts:

1. *Trust A*, also known as a "marital trust" or "Wife's trust," would be for the sole benefit of Mrs. Wilson and could cover at least $200,000 of her assets.
2. *Trust B*, a "family trust," would take care of the remaining assets but not more than $600,000 in assets.

Under Trust A, Mrs. Wilson would receive at least the income of the estate during her lifetime and, usually, portions of the principal. Lawyers use language such as: "My wife may have as much principal as is needed for her care, maintenance, and support." Translated, this means that she should be allowed to have what she needs to maintain the standard of living to which she is accustomed. The trust could then provide that on the death of Mrs. Wilson any amount left in the trust would go to the children of Mr. and Mrs. Wilson. There is no need that there be a Trust A. The $200,000 could go outright to Mrs. Wilson at Mr. Wilson's death.

Under Trust B, the widow usually receives the income for her life, and additional principal which may be necessary for her support (after the principal in Trust A has been exhausted). At her death, the remaining principal in Trust B will usually go to the couple's children. Income and principal of Trust B could also be available for the couple's children—or, if Mrs. Wilson has sufficient assets of her own, might even go to the children when Mr. Wilson dies.

None of the assets in Trust B will become a part of Mrs. Wilson's taxable estate because the Personal Representative of Mr. Wilson's estate did not select Trust B assets to qualify for the marital deduction. Generally, the administration of such trusts is best accomplished by a third party.

The result of this type of planning is that if Mrs. Wilson in her own right has $400,000 of assets, then on her subsequent death, the only assets that would be subject to the federal estate tax would be these assets plus the Trust A assets of $200,000. The total then would be $600,000, the maximum exemption equivalent (1987). The result is that there would be no federal estate tax on the death of Mrs. Wilson. The Wilsons were able to pass a total of $1,200,000 to their children free and clear of any federal estate tax.

No one can ever be certain as to exactly how much they will be worth when they die. Estate planning is accomplished by the use of formulas that will achieve maximum saving results.

STATE DEATH TAXES

Don't forget that you may have to pay state death and gift taxes (especially when substantial assets are involved) even if, in some cases, you don't have to pay a federal estate or gift tax. States may require a complete accounting regardless of the size of the estate. It's not unusual for a state inheritance or estate tax to be imposed even though no federal estate tax is due.

REVIEW BY THE IRS

All federal estate tax returns are audited by the Internal Revenue Service. Usually the depth of the review is related to the size and complexity of the estate. The simplest review is a desk audit made by the IRS office without the presence of a representative of the executor. Large estates, or estates belonging to persons who over the years have reported little income, are given more detailed scrutiny.

Generally, property received by inheritance is not subject to income tax—federal, state, or municipal. Nor need the money or property you inherit be reported on your annual personal income tax return. However, there *are* taxes on the income or appreciation later realized on such property.

According to a legal maxim, there are two federal estate taxes: one for people who have planned their estate, the other for those who have failed to plan properly. There can be vast differences between the two levies.

Even if you have a modest estate, you will find it worth your while to start financial planning early in life. Planning can save money on taxes while you live and after you die. You will find the small cost of professional counsel to be far more than repaid in tax savings, plus added security and happiness for your loved ones.

REMEMBER

1. The new Tax Act substantially changed the manner and amount of death tax levies.
2. If your estate plan has not been reviewed by an estate planning attorney since the new law was enacted in 1981, you should seek review and advice immediately.
3. If you are married, your attorney will probably suggest you take advantage of the unlimited marital deduction; and if the assets of you and your spouse exceed the exemption equivalent amount, tax-saving trust(s) may be suggested.
4. Without this arrangement, your estate may pay substantially increased taxes and your children will receive less than they would have received had proper planning been accomplished.

ESTATE AND INHERITANCE TAXES

Table No. 1 UNIFIED TRANSFER TAX RATE SCHEDULE
FOR
1982

If the amount is: Over	But not over	Tax	Tentative tax* is: + %	On Excess Over
$ 0	$ 10,000	$ 0	18	$ 0
10,000	20,000	1,800	20	10,000
20,000	40,000	3,800	22	20,000
40,000	60,000	8,200	24	40,000
60,000	80,000	13,000	26	60,000
80,000	100,000	18,200	28	80,000
100,000	150,000	23,800	30	100,000
150,000	250,000	38,800	32	150,000
250,000	500,000	70,800	34	250,000
500,000	750,000	155,800	37	500,000
750,000	1,000,000	248,300	39	750,000
1,000,000	1,250,000	345,800	41	1,000,000
1,250,000	1,500,000	448,300	43	1,250,000
1,500,000	2,000,000	555,800	45	1,500,000
2,000,000	2,500,000	780,800	49	2,000,000
2,500,000	3,000,000	1,025,800	53	2,500,000
3,000,000	3,500,000	1,290,800	57	3,000,000
3,500,000	4,000,000	1,575,800	61	3,500,000
4,000,000		1,880,800	65	4,000,000

1982 Unified Credit: $64,000

*The cumulated transfers to which the tentative tax applies are the sum of (a) the amount of the taxable estate and (b) the amount of the taxable gifts made by the decedent after 1976 other than gifts includible in the gross estate.

Table No. 2 UNIFIED TRANSFER TAX RATE SCHEDULE
FOR
1983

If the amount is: Over	But not over	Tax	Tentative tax* is: + %	On Excess Over
$ 0	$ 10,000	$ 0	18	$ 0
10,000	20,000	1,800	20	10,000
20,000	40,000	3,800	22	20,000
40,000	60,000	8,200	24	40,000
60,000	80,000	13,000	26	60,000
80,000	100,000	18,200	28	80,000
100,000	150,000	23,800	30	100,000
150,000	250,000	38,800	32	150,000
250,000	500,000	70,800	34	250,000
500,000	750,000	155,800	37	500,000
750,000	1,000,000	248,300	39	750,000
1,000,000	1,250,000	345,800	41	1,000,000
1,250,000	1,500,000	448,300	43	1,250,000
1,500,000	2,000,000	555,800	45	1,500,000
2,000,000	2,500,000	780,800	49	2,000,000
2,500,000	3,000,000	1,025,800	53	2,500,000
3,000,000	3,500,000	1,290,800	57	3,000,000
3,500,000		1,575,800	60	3,500,000

1983 Unified Credit: $77,300

*The cumulated transfers to which the tentative tax applies are the sum of (a) the amount of the taxable estate and (b) the amount of the taxable gifts made by the decedent after 1976 other than gifts includible in the gross estate.

ESTATE AND INHERITANCE TAXES

Table No. 3 UNIFIED TRANSFER TAX RATE SCHEDULE
FOR
1984

If the amount is: Over	But not over	Tax	Tentative tax* is: + %	On Excess Over
$ 0	$ 10,000	$ 0	18	$ 0
10,000	20,000	1,800	20	10,000
20,000	40,000	3,800	22	20,000
40,000	60,000	8,200	24	40,000
60,000	80,000	13,000	26	60,000
80,000	100,000	18,200	28	80,000
100,000	150,000	23,800	30	100,000
150,000	250,000	38,800	32	150,000
250,000	500,000	70,800	34	250,000
500,000	750,000	155,800	37	500,000
750,000	1,000,000	248,300	39	750,000
1,000,000	1,250,000	345,800	41	1,000,000
1,250,000	1,500,000	448,300	43	1,250,000
1,500,000	2,000,000	555,800	45	1,500,000
2,000,000	2,500,000	780,800	49	2,000,000
2,500,000	3,000,000	1,025,800	53	2,500,000
3,000,000		1,290,800	55	3,000,000

1984 Unified Credit is: $96,300

*The cumulated transfers to which the tentative tax applies are the sum of (a) the amount of the taxable estate and (b) the amount of the taxable gifts made by the decedent after 1976 other than gifts includible in the gross estate.

Table No. 4 UNIFIED TRANSFER TAX RATE SCHEDULE
FOR
1985 AND THEREAFTER

If the amount is: Over	But not over	Tax	Tentative tax* is: + %	On Excess Over
$ 0	$ 10,000	$ 0	18	$ 0
10,000	20,000	1,800	20	10,000
20,000	40,000	3,800	22	20,000
40,000	60,000	8,200	24	40,000
60,000	80,000	13,000	26	60,000
80,000	100,000	18,200	28	80,000
100,000	150,000	23,800	30	100,000
150,000	250,000	38,800	32	150,000
250,000	500,000	70,800	34	250,000
500,000	750,000	155,800	37	500,000
750,000	1,000,000	248,300	39	750,000
1,000,000	1,250,000	345,800	41	1,000,000
1,250,000	1,500,000	448,300	43	1,250,000
1,500,000	2,000,000	555,800	45	1,500,000
2,000,000	2,500,000	780,800	49	2,000,000
2,500,000		1,025,800	50	2,500,000

1985 Unified Credit is: $121,800
1986 Unified Credit is: $155,800
1987 Unified Credit is: $192,700

*The cumulated transfers to which the tentative tax applies are the sum of (a) the amount of the taxable estate and (b) the amount of the taxable gifts made by the decedent after 1976 other than gifts includible in the gross estate.

ESTATE AND INHERITANCE TAXES

Table No. 5

The Federal law provides a credit against the Federal Estate Tax for State Death taxes. The credit is as follows:

COMPUTATION OF MAXIMUM CREDIT FOR STATE DEATH TAXES
(Based on Federal adjusted taxable estate which is the
Federal taxable estate reduced by $60,000)

Adjusted taxable estate equal to or more than (1)	Adjusted taxable estate less than (2)	Credit on amount in column (1) (3)	Rate of credit on excess over amount in column (1) (4)
0	40,000	0	None
40,000	90,000	0	0.8
90,000	140,000	400	1.6
140,000	240,000	1,200	2.4
240,000	440,000	3,600	3.2
440,000	640,000	10,000	4.0
640,000	840,000	18,000	4.8
840,000	1,040,000	27,600	5.6
1,040,000	1,540,000	38,800	6.4
1,540,000	2,040,000	70,800	7.2
2,040,000	2,540,000	106,800	8.0
2,540,000	3,040,000	146,800	8.8
3,040,000	3,540,000	190,800	9.6
3,540,000	4,040,000	238,800	10.4
4,040,000	5,040,000	290,800	11.2
5,040,000	6,040,000	402,800	12.0
6,040,000	7,040,000	522,800	12.8
7,040,000	8,040,000	650,800	13.6
8,040,000	9,040,000	786,800	14.4
9,040,000	10,040,000	930,800	15.2
10,040,000		1,082,800	16.0

In determining the total death tax payable, a decedent's estate will pay at least these amounts to the State death tax authorities and if the State does not have a death tax (e.g. Nevada) there will be no State credit given and the Federal Government will keep the entire tax payable as shown on Tables 1, 2, 3 or 4.

Table No. 6

After giving effect to the State Death tax credit (see Table No. 5) the net federal estate tax is relatively unprogressive as shown by the following table which reflects the net estate tax payable in 1987 and thereafter:

Amount transferred	Effective federal rate
Up to $600,000	0
$600,001 to $750,000	32.2
$750,000 to $800,000	34.2
$800,000 to $1,000,000	33.4
$1,000,000 to $1,250,000	34.6
$1,250,000 to $1,500,000	36.6
$1,500,000 to $2,000,000	37.8
$2,000,000 to $2,500,000	41.0
$2,500,000 to $3,000,000	41.2
$3,000,000 to $3,500,000	40.4
$3,500,000 to $4,000,000	36.6
$4,000,000 to $5,000,000	38.8
$5,000,000 to $6,000,000	38.0
$6,000,000 to $7,000,000	37.2
$7,000,000 to $8,000,000	36.4
$8,000,000 to $9,000,000	35.6
$9,000,000 to $10,000,000	34.8
$10,000,000 +	34.0

7

Estate planning

Estate planning refers to the thoughtful arrangement of one's affairs and the disposition of one's property with the assistance of technical experts. It has as its basic purposes to meet an individual's objectives in life and to ensure attainment of specific goals for beneficiaries after the planner's death.

It is not a do-it-yourself, once-over-lightly process. A successful estate plan involves a thorough review of one's current assets and future prospects, and requires the expertise of a skilled attorney as well as, often, an insurance agent, a trust officer, and an accountant. It is feasible to start your own estate planning, but without proper counsel, your hopes may be frustrated and your beneficiaries may have to face seemingly endless difficulties.

Here are the basic steps you can take to set yourself on the right path for effective estate planning.

Take inventory. List *all* your assets: your home, furniture, automobile, jewelry, savings and checking accounts, your share in employee benefit plans, securities, real estate, life insurance, and anything else of value. A full, accurate inventory will give you an idea of what should be done, what has to be accomplished in the future, and how you should distribute your estate among your family and loved ones. It will also help your attorney and other advisers to implement your wishes wisely, with a view to minimum tax liability and the greatest protection now and in the future.

Insofar as possible, the inventories should be compiled in cooperation with your spouse and—when they are old enough—your children.

Since the legal documents needed to set up your plan rarely mention specific assets or their values, it's satisfactory to approximate the total worth. It is, however, of paramount importance to determine the title to each item, the date of its acquisition, and the cost at that time. Questions to be asked in the process of taking inventory include:

- Is your real estate held in joint tenancy? If so, with whom?
- Are securities held in joint tenancy? If so, with whom?
- Are assets held in your name only?
- Who is the beneficiary of your life insurance and does the beneficiary receive the death proceeds outright or in installments?
- Provisions of any divorce decrees?
- Provisions of buy/sell or other business agreements/stock options?

Accuracy is important in answering such questions, so examine each bankbook, stock certificate, insurance policy, real estate deed, and any other item very carefully. Unless you have acquired considerable wealth, there's no need to hire an appraiser, but for tax purposes it's a good idea to have two figures for real estate and securities: *the date of their acquisition and their value at that time*.

The Estate Information and Inventory forms on pages 121-132 should assist you in taking an initial inventory and then updating it annually. Note that these pages are perforated. When completed, they can be removed and brought with you to your first interview with your attorney.

After adding all your assets and subtracting all your liabilities, you will get your net worth: the net amount of your estate at the time of inventory.

Keep everything up to date annually. A business has a financial statement prepared yearly—so should you.

Keep your projections flexible. If you or anyone else in your family stands to inherit property, benefit from a trust fund, or gain other assets, add the likely sum to the proper column with an asterisk (*). This is to indicate that you are not including such possibilities of wealth in your primary calculations, but will consider them in determining your estate plan.

Spell out your objectives. Be clear about your objectives in order to provide the framework needed by your advisers. As you plan your estate, focus on what might happen in the event of your death. What provision do you want to make for your spouse? For the children?

Think of what would happen if there were a disaster which took the lives of both parents or even one parent and the children?

Keep in mind that your will and your estate will survive you. Their effects will be felt by your spouse, your children, and, possibly, your grandchildren throughout their lifetimes. A will or estate plan that may engender bitterness runs counter to the objectives of sound estate planning, which is to add happiness and economic security for your loved ones' future prospects.

Make your plan for the long term. Even if you feel that each child in the family is different—let's say one of them is a spendthrift—think carefully before you make any special provisions. Treating one child differently may do him more harm than good, not only in relation to his happiness (how he remembers you and regards your attitude toward him), but also because it may influence his future ability to handle property.

Responsible management of money and property is difficult to learn without actual experience. Years ago, well-to-do fathers customarily established lifetime provisions for their daughters. The father, not quite certain that a daughter would make a "good" marriage, thus ensured continuing support for her. Or a father who was worried that his son would gamble might limit him to the income from his inheritance. However, such practices are seldom relevant to today's changed circumstances and so are rarely used.

Common sense should play the biggest role in setting your objectives. For example, you should be aware that if your wife survives you and your children are minors, the value of your estate will probably undergo a strain, especially with ever rising costs of college and other post-high school training. Furthermore, if the children are very young, they will need the mother's guidance, so that it may be difficult for her to undertake a career. If she does work, there will be the extra expenses of day care for the children.

The number one concern of most married men is their wives. Notwithstanding ERA and changing womens' roles in society, husbands feel a continuing responsibility for their wives and with good reason. The children will grow up and leave to get married and pursue their own careers. In many cases, however, the wife will find herself out of touch with the job market and, due to age and lack of employable skills, will have difficulty in securing adequately paid employment.

In most families, the husband undertakes the responsibility of trying to build and plan his estate to provide reasonable lifetime security for the woman who became his marriage partner. This does not mean that an estate plan should be for the wife's exclusive benefit. If the resources of the estate are substantial enough, some funds should also be made available to the children during their mother's lifetime.

Such provisions could be in the form of direct bequests or funds held in trust; the terms of the trust would depend upon the size of the estate and the needs and maturity of the children. There is no reason why assets should not be used to help children pay for postgraduate education, start a business, or acquire a homestead. So when you have provided adequate protection for your wife, consider in what ways your property can bring the greatest happiness to your children or grandchildren.

Set up the plan. Once you know your assets and have defined your objectives, the next step is to implement your plan. To do this, you will need to choose people who will now advise you further and explain to you how best to carry out your program.

At this point, you may be discouraged and you may fear that your estate is not large enough to do the job you have in mind. The single best solution for someone in this situation is life insurance. A good insurance agent can help you to bring your estate up to a point at which it will adequately support your widow and children while they are still dependents.

Life insurance comes in all sizes and shapes, but the basic purpose is "death" protection: to provide money at the death of the insured. Upon proof of the death of a policyholder, the insurance company pays a predetermined sum (the face value of the policy plus accumulations, if any, minus any outstanding loans) to the designated

ESTATE PLANNING

beneficiary or beneficiaries. This provides ready money to meet the financial needs of the heirs.

There are two general categories of life insurance:

1. *Straight life.* This kind of insurance builds cash values with the payment of premiums larger than needed to assure protection alone. Over the years, there is a slow, steady increase in the assets (cash value). This can be important in estate planning, because this money becomes the basis for borrowing or, through dividends earned on the investment of these funds, reduces the annual carrying costs.
2. *Term life.* This insurance, which provides protection but builds no cash value, is strictly a death benefit. Generally, term life insurance is sold for a short period of time, five or ten years, and can then be renewed at a higher premium. One of its great advantages is that it can be used to create an "instant" estate when you are young and have not accumulated substantial wealth. As the children grow older and are able to earn money on their own, the amount of money needed for their support becomes smaller and you can afford to drop some of the term life coverage.

    A cheaper form of protection is known as "decreasing term life insurance." This insurance is widely used with mortgages because its terms provide that the death payment decreases as the equity in the home increases—for example, a twenty-year mortgage of $70,000 would be balanced by a $70,000 decreasing term life policy. As the mortgage is amortized, the value of the insurance drops proportionately and disappears with the last mortgage payment.

Think of the role of your wife in handling the estate. One of the most frequently asked questions we have heard in helping plan an estate is: "How much freedom should be given my wife?"

In most cases, we answer, "Plenty." Many husbands fear leaving their wives in complete control of the property. They think that, especially if their wives become widows while still young and of marriageable age, they will be duped or conned. The fact is that most widows who lose any of their inheritance do so by error of omission rather than by commission. These ladies are cautious, often overly so. Sometimes a situation does arise in which a widow is beguiled by "brother Charley and his get-rich-quick schemes." However, the more typical widow is so chary about outside advice that she generally disregards all counsel, and that sometimes includes the advice of competent persons given responsibilities by her husband.

As a general rule, we advise that the wife take an active part in estate planning: in the inventory, in outlining objectives, and in the development of the will and the establishment of trusts. We also suggest that the husband give his widow considerable freedom in handling the estate. And above all, make sure she understands and participates to the fullest in the estate planning.

The husband should concentrate on chosing competent advisers and in planning to leave his property in such a way that, on his death, these advisers automatically appear on the scene and are prepared to help the widow and children.

Where both spouses work. The preceding portions of this chapter have been devoted for the most part to situations where the male member of the household has been the breadwinner.

In young America today, it is the exception, rather than the rule, when the male is the sole breadwinner. Statistics show that today in young marriage situations, nearly all wives work—and often it is many years after marriage before children come along and sometimes never. In fact, from time to time, there are situations where the female of the marriage does better financially than the male.

From an estate planning viewpoint, this type of situation—until children come along—does not present a great problem. If either spouse dies, the other really has no problem of support. He or she has already demonstrated this capability.

In marriages without children where both spouses work, the trend today seems to be to "spend everything." They seem to forget that the day may come along when they will have to live on only one salary. Sometimes the best estate planning advice that can be given couples of this type is financial advice. Pay yourself first. Put regular sums away. So simple, yet so difficult.

Where there are children involved, it is always quite clear that the parents want whatever there is, if both are deceased, to be used for the care and maintenance of the children.

In marriages without children, the concern is what will happen to whatever estate has been built up after both parties die. If the parties have not carefully attended to details, it well could develop that one side of the family would get everything.

For instance, say a young man, recently married and with no children dies without a will, leaving everything to his wife, and within a few days she, too, dies—perhaps the result of a common accident. In most states, all the wealth they had accumulated, even if recently given to the young man by his relatives, would pass to his surviving wife, and on her death all her wealth would go to her side of the family. This could produce a very unfair situation. The family of the first to die had a hand in creating the wealth of the parties, but because no planning had taken place, everything was left to the family of the last to die. With proper planning, all this could have been avoided.

ESTATE PLANNING FOR SINGLES

Obviously, unmarried persons should give careful thought to the planning of their estates. Although many single persons do not have dependents or persons who regularly receive support and financial assistance from them, they should have an interest in seeing that in the event of death, their estates are distributed to those persons and organizations they wish to benefit and with a minimum tax cost and administrative expense. While outright distribution from a simple will may be appropriate for parents, brothers, sisters, and recognized charities, the use of trusts should also be considered. An aged parent or a minor niece or nephew would make an excellent case for the use of a trust under will.

Older singles who do not have spouses or children to assist them with the administration of their financial affairs should consider the creation of an inter vivos trust, so that if their abilities to administer their financial affairs should diminish severely, their trustee will be ready to assume the tasks.

It has been our experience that most single persons with children, whether by divorce or by death of a spouse, are especially concerned about what will happen to the children if he or she dies. Accordingly, plans are made. The plan usually results in a trust arrangement for the children if they are minors.

There has been a great deal of recent publicity about unmarried persons who live together, sometimes sharing a homestead, oftentimes sharing expenses and income as well. Obviously, it is important from a legal point of view that these parties receive competent legal and tax advice. Generally speaking, most state laws do not recognize a common-law marital relationship. Thus, the surviving partner would receive no inheritance at law—i.e., in situations where the decedent died without a will. Unmarried persons who desire to leave their estates or a portion of their property to an unmarried partner should have a properly drawn will providing for such a distribution. Without this, the surviving partner would have to base his or her claim on some form of contract. If a written agreement does not exist, the survivor's chances of receiving anything are poor. This is a developing area of law and it is extremely important that persons who find themselves in these circumstances receive competent legal advice.

SECOND MARRIAGES

The number of divorced and widowed persons who remarry is substantial. From an estate planning point of view, their circumstances often differ from those marrying for the first time. In many cases, there are separate estates and separate families and sometimes minor children. The second marriage may present a conflict of motives: a desire to provide care for the surviving spouse but also to recognize the interests of children born of the prior marriage. Many enter the second marriage without giving thought to this serious topic, only to find themselves later in a legal predicament.

It is extremely important that one receive competent legal advice *before* undertaking the second marriage. It is probable that the lawyer dealing with such a case will recommend that the parties enter into a prenuptial or antenuptial agreement. Such an agree-

ESTATE PLANNING

ment will usually specify separate assets and estates and their separate intentions as to distribution on death. A well-drawn antenuptial agreement overrides state laws requiring distribution to surviving spouses.

There are several pitfalls in this area, among them:

1. Not recognizing the need for such an agreement until after the marriage. The enforceability of agreements entered after marriage is not clear in many states, and in fact such postnuptial agreements may be unenforceable. This underlines the importance of making the agreement prior to the second marriage ceremony.
2. Each party should consult his or her own attorney. There is a natural conflict of interest between parties entering into an antenuptial agreement and it is almost impossible for one attorney to properly represent both parties. The emotions of those contemplating marriage do not usually lend themselves to separate legal consultation—but this should be undertaken.

OWNERSHIP OF PROPERTY IN MORE THAN ONE STATE

We are a mobile society and more and more people are acquiring property, usually a vacation home, in a state other than their state of residence. Often this means that on the death of the owner there must be two parallel probate proceedings: one in the state of residence and the other in the state in which the property is located. This almost always adds to the total cost of probating the decedent's estate and thus should be avoided if practicable. This "extra" probate is sometimes referred to as an ancillary probate.

One of the best ways of avoiding a double probate is through the prudent use of joint tenancy where the owners are married to each other; or through the use of a partnership entity to hold title. On occasion, a revocable trust could even be used.

8

The role of the lawyer and estate planning aides

In estate planning, your lawyer is the key person. He is the "captain" of the team, which, depending on the scope of your assets, may include a trust officer, an insurance agent, an accountant, and an investment adviser.

Your lawyer, by training and tradition, should have one primary obligation—*to you, his client*. He strives to give each client the full benefit of his knowledge and experience; ideally, he will advise against something he feels is not in your best interest and carefully scrutinize all proposals and provide impartial counsel.

He is in the best position to make the required suggestions, to ask the required questions, and to render the required judgments, because his income and continued success as a professional depend on his having the proper expertise and having served only you, his client. The attorney who helps in planning your estate should have no incentive to spend or invest your money. His compensation should be set by a predetermined, though not necessarily fixed, fee arrangement, usually on an hourly basis.

Before discussing how to choose a lawyer, let's review the other people who can be helpful in estate planning. How important they might be to you will depend on the size of your estate, your family responsibilities, and what you wish to be done after your death. Some lawyers who are specialists in estate planning and probate sometimes resent and even oppose outside assistance, but we think this is an unjustified attitude. In more than forty years of joint experience, we have found that the majority of lawyers "partners" in estate planning are concerned, helpful, and anxious to serve the best interests of their clients. Generally, there are four of them:

Trust officer. The executives of most trust companies conduct themselves in a professional manner and try to produce the best results for each client. Whether this is due to altruism or the desire to preserve the institution's reputation for integrity, thereby maintaining its competitive status, is of no practical importance. A professional trustee can render valuable service.

Life insurance agent. Whether you have a little or a lot of insurance, a life insurance agent should be involved in your estate planning. He does have a selfish motive in that his income depends upon the sale of insurance, but life insurance is nevertheless important to a family at all stages. It provides protection for a young family; it assures a balanced investment program during middle age; and it makes possible tax savings and security at retirement.

In recent years, no industry has done more to invoke professional standards and performance in its sales force than the life insurance industry. The designation CLU (Chartered Life Underwriter) is held only by those who have undergone extensive training in various aspects of estate planning and who have successfully passed a series of written examinations. We have found that most people with the CLU designation are competent, professional, and able to provide worthwhile advice.

Investment adviser. It often is advisable to have a firm or an individual as an investment adviser if your estate consists of a number of securities or business investments. If you prefer to handle your own money while you live, you should make arrangements for your estate representative to retain counsel. As outlined earlier, do not hesitate to designate an investment adviser to work with the bank or trust company responsible for handling your estate or trust.

Accountant. Many persons, especially those who are in business, rely greatly on the advice of their accountant. These advisers are often the best source of financial data in an estate planning case. An accountant who is a CPA (Certified Public Accountant) has received special training and experience and has passed a difficult qualifying examination.

CHOOSING YOUR LAWYER

Selecting an attorney to help you in estate planning is a serious and often a difficult task. The average person does not even know a lawyer. Occasionally, he is the guy next door who says "Hi" over the fence—or a high school classmate whose firm's office is next door to the bank. You have no way of knowing whether such an individual can draft a good plan or advise you properly.

Approval of advertising by lawyers is so recent that only a few attorneys have utilized this form of public information. In most cases, when you seek legal cousel, you must rely on recommendations and reputation.

One source for recommendations could be your insurance agent, especially if he works in the estate planning area. Keep in mind, however, that that does not necessarily mean he will be a good judge of legal competence.

You can also inquire at your bank. Must trust departments have estate planning divisions that work with local attorneys, and their experience in dealing with both customers and lawyers can be useful. Furthermore, some states and large cities have bar reference organizations with whom many qualified attorneys register; such an organization may provide a starting point for recommendations.

However you make your selection, check the individual and his firm carefully. You are hiring someone who will be intimately involved with your future—for many years, you hope. Usually, a family lawyer should be able to handle estate planning. That's one of the reasons for engaging a family lawyer in the first place. But when your property is large or diverse, you may need a specialist. He should then supplement, not replace, your family attorney.

A good family lawyer can give you and your loved ones peace of mind just by being available. He can save you dollars by preventing you from making a costly mistake. He can provide counsel during negotiations and litigation and support in a family crisis such as death.

Approach the selection of your lawyer as you would any business proposition. But most important, make sure he is working only for you and only in your best interests and those of your family. Set down the specific needs you have, and once you have narrowed down your list of candidates, take the following steps:

1. Call for an appointment. When you call, explain your purpose. In most cases, there will be a charge.
2. Be frank in explaining your resources and hopes and in asking about the lawyer's view on investments, counseling your heirs, and the use of trusts.

    Expertise is important, but you want your widow and children to feel comfortable with the individual you select. Therefore, it's a good idea to bring your spouse along. The meeting will establish a relationship and give the attorney a chance to explain some of the legal requirements involved in planning an estate and what probate is all about.
3. Ask about charges. For estate planning, charges are usually based on time spent. To secure all the facts and properly counsel a client and draft the proper instrument takes time, and time and effort are essentials of the lawyer's product. How often a new client will say, "All I want is a simple will. How much do you charge?" There's a lot more to a responsible job of estate planning than just preparing a will.
4. Look for integrity. By tradition and statute, lawyers have been accorded special privileges and responsibilities. The great majority of them try to maintain high standards, but as in any profession, there are some whose efforts are more geared toward rewarding themselves than serving their clients. Often, such lawyers are good salesmen but poor advisers, especially when confronted with the complexities of estate planning. However, the danger of selecting a lawyer who misrepresents his expertise is lessening as more "victims" file—and win—malpractice suits based on the results of so-called estate planning.

Beware of the lawyer who says that he (or she) will prepare a "simple will" for $35. There is no way a competent job of estate planning and all the counseling that should go into it can be accomplished for such a charge. You may get the $35 will—but that's all you get. Your search for economy may in the end be very expensive.

Drafting a will or trust agreement comes only after thorough analysis, which often results in recommendations for rearranging your holdings to assure a sound, economical long-term program. In other words, it's what happens *before* the preparation of an instrument that takes much of the time.

PROBATE FEES

In the past, state laws set legal fees for the probate of estates on a percentage basis. The fees were the same for easy-to-handle and for relatively complicated estates. Today, enlightened leaders of the legal profession, mindful of the possibility that such fee schedules might restrict competition and anxious to assure charges that are fair to both client and lawyer, recommend charges based upon the work involved, and this normally is on an hourly basis. Figured this way, the fee would then reflect the time involved and the complexity of the estate.

In most cases, probate fees are modest and will not significantly reduce estate assets. They are lowest when the will has been properly drawn and kept up to date, and there has been continuing estate planning. But the charges can escalate when an estate that at first glance appeared routine turns out to involve unreported obligations of the decedent or difficulties develop in administration or disposition of estate assets.

Because of the frequent changes in laws and the spread of special benefits such as retirement plans, the preparation of a will and other estate planning documents is becoming increasingly difficult. That's another reason it pays to start the process early and review one's situation frequently.

Many people are reluctant to accept the cost of estate planning because:

 1. Estate planning involves the unpleasant subject of death.

2. In large measure, it relates to something beyond the client's lifetime and to tax savings that will benefit someone else.
3. It is frustrating and, in terms of human nature and usual purchasing habits, uncharacteristic to commit oneself to anything for which there is no sure cost.

Yet lawyers must be compensated for their time and skill. Conceiving and implementing a worthwhile estate plan takes many hours, in which basic data are gathered, alternative recommendations considered, the necessary documents prepared, and the reasons for and terms of the plan explained to the client and his family.

To those unfamiliar with the details of the legal process, the delays that occur in court procedures, and the impact of changes in laws, the fees may seem large. But they represent the time spent—usually months, often years. As pointed out before, in many cases the current fees will be more than offset by future savings.

Estate planning today takes a great deal of skill. Lawyers spend countless hours at seminars and reading the ever changing laws and court decisions that result in changing strategies. In short, it is hardwork.

Few attorneys are able, or find it possible, to set a definite price in advance, especially if they have not had a chance to spend some time with the prospective client and to learn some of the facts of his estate. To expect a lawyer to commit himself on a fee for estate planning is comparable to asking a garage mechanic the cost of repairs before he has examined the damage to the car.

Our experience in the field and our contacts with other estate planners lead us to believe that the best way to handle the problem of proper fees is to have frank discussions on the subject at the beginning of the relationship and regularly over the years. The client has the right to get the lawyer's best estimate of fees and costs for planning and probate.

Our advice: Ask that your attorney set a range within which he expects the charges to fall. In most cases, the final bill will be fairly close to his quotation, but if unusual situations occur or if you change your mind on the disposition of assets, costs will probably be higher.

Once, after due consideration, you have selected your lawyer, you must have confidence that the person you have chosen is an honest, dedicated professional who will do the best job at a reasonable price. After all, legal fees are insignificant if your estate is planned to meet your objectives.

One final point: Do not delay in making a change if, for some reason, you become convinced that you made an error in your choice. Your relationship with your lawyer should be a long-term satisfactory one, and if you feel you have made a mistake, make a change.

REVIEWING ESTATE PLANNING

Estate planning is a never-ending process. Just because you have completed your plan, written a will, and signed various documents, it doesn't mean you can forget your program. Estate plans deal with the future, and so they are subject to change and adjustment.

It is advisable to review your plan every couple of years, preferably with your attorney, and when called for, with other members of your advisory team. Reviewing the plan involves going over the basic documents to see whether they still "fit" or whether changes in your own or your family situation suggest revisions. Every three or four years, you may find it helpful to recalculate your estate and redefine your objectives. This reassessment is especially important if you have inherited money or advanced to a more remunerative position, and if previously dependent young members of the family have become independent or older relatives have become more dependent on you—in short, if there have been any substantial changes in your financial picture.

The purpose of the review is to make certain that your plan is still viable. If it is not, make the necessary adjustments immediately.

One very important time to check your plan is at retirement, when you, and possibly also your spouse, can start getting social security checks or withdrawing benefits from your pension or profit-sharing plan.

Once you have this kind of assured monthly income, you might be in a position to revise your bequests and to start making gifts. All changes should be made within the broad framework of your total estate plan and only after careful consideration of your own needs, of adequate protection for your spouse, and of the financial future of your heirs. Keep in mind that illness in your family may be costly. The money you counted on for a worry-free retirement can be rapidly depleted. And once a gift has been made, there is almost no way to make the beneficiary responsible for proper care of you and your spouse. An experienced lawyer can earn his fee through the counsel he gives at retirement time alone.

9

Choosing trustees and estate administrators

CHOOSING A TRUSTEE

Almost anyone, including the person who establishes the trust (the donor or trustor), can serve as a trustee. It's a fact of life that the one establishing the trust will probably have the greatest interest in and devotion to the trust, but it may not always be practical for him to assume the responsibility. Also, certain tax objectives may not be obtainable if the one establishing the trust also acts as the trustee of it. And of course, there are those most frequent occasions when trusts are established in wills, to become effective after the death of the creator of the will (the testator).

Until recent times, most trustees were individuals, usually relatives or friends. But as the business of property management became more specialized, more trustees are professionals, typically employees of a bank or trust company. Their fees usually are expressed as a percentage of the assets in the trust. Trust business can be profitable, so there is competition—a fact to remember when you make your choice of a trustee.

Note: When you consider appointing an institution as trustee, be sure the fees are not too high in relation to your trust assets. Most banks have an annual minimum fee of at least $500 and sometimes there are termination fees. Be sure to find out exactly what fees will be charged. When holdings are small, you'll be better off to name a relative or friend.

There are advantages to naming a relative as trustee. For example, you can know that your brother-in-law is familiar with your financial affairs, understands why the trust was created, and has a good relationship with the beneficiaries. Furthermore, he will probably serve for little or no remuneration.

But there are problems with such arrangements:

1. Individuals are mortal. A trustee may die before the end of the trust or become disabled or incapable of handling business matters or making business decisions. It's best to name an alternate trustee at the outset. That way, if for any reason your brother-in-law is unable to act, the alternative person has already been nominated.

An institution, on the other hand, does not become ill or incapacitated and is likely to continue in business. Furthermore, you can get special services such as computer readouts, property management, and portfolio analysis.

2. The interest of an individual trustee may wane if the compensation is not adequate. Whether or not he is a member of the family, a trustee has the right to a fair-value payment for services rendered. The saying "You get what you pay for" is applicable in this situation.

You can get extra services by paying special fees to professionals who can call on their institution's specialized skills and facilities, such as computers. But the individual trustee who performs effectively is well worth the money he requests. He should be paid and the trust instrument should so state.

3. A relative may lack the necessary skills. A relative, though he might be a fine schoolteacher, might not be able to handle a $500,000 trust fund for your widow or heirs. He might simply lack the right experience or temperament for the job.

Many intelligent people have little knowledge of money and property. When a wife and children request funds, the trustee must be able to sort out those needs that are worthwhile and make allocations in keeping with the intentions of the person who established the trust.

An inexperienced trustee will get on-the-job training at the donor's expense. A few mistakes or inefficient administration can be costly and irritating.

4. The financial responsibility of a relative may not be impeccable. Uncle Joe may be a wonderful fellow, but he may cause the trust to go broke, and he too goes broke—and then there's no way to get back any money lost through his poor administration. This problem doesn't exist with the corporate fiduciary; it has the resources to pay for possible negligence.

5. *A relative may become unavailable because of business or personal commitments.* If cousin Bill retires to California, he will not be able to properly supervise a trust in Maine. Or if the trustee has to travel a good deal, he may not be able to spend the time needed to manage the property or to tend promptly to the needs of the beneficiaries.

An institution will not move away and will always have people who are ready to help. The costs to you may be higher, but they are likely to be reasonable because of competition and supervision by the courts.

6. *Taxes must be considered.* Trusts more often than not are established for tax reasons. The general idea is to give beneficiaries economic benefits from the property held in trust—but in such a way as to not cause the property held in trust to be considered a part of the beneficiary's taxable estate when the beneficiary dies. For this reason, and sometimes for income tax reasons, it is advisable, and sometimes necessary, that one who in no way is a beneficiary be the trustee of the trust.

7. *Impartiality is often desirable.* Trustees sometimes are called upon to make difficult or unpopular decisions. In divided family situations, often the beneficiaries feel more comfortable if a "neutral" makes the decisions. There are those times when a surviving spouse would like to say "no" to a financial request from a relative; how convenient it is to be able to say, "The bank is handling my affairs; you will have to ask the bank." Usually, that is the last of such requests.

It has been our experience that, as a general rule, an individual trustee is satisfactory for a small trust under $100,000 but an institution may be more effective when the assets are greater and involve special management problems or hard-to-please beneficiaries.

CHOOSING AN EXECUTOR

The executor (designated "personal representative" in some states) is the individual or organization responsible for administering your estate. In general, the qualifications needed for executor are similiar to those required of a trustee: availability, integrity, administrative ability, financial responsibility, and empathy with the heirs. Executors have great responsibilities. The executor should be selected with great care. The executor will be the one that "runs the show" after you are gone! Their duties are called for when you are no longer living—no longer around to "fire" them.

By law, the function of the personal representative is to fulfill the testator's written wishes to complete the steps mandated for an accounting of the disposition of the estate to the beneficiaries, the tax authorities, and the probate court. In the process, he is trying to match the intentions of the deceased with the needs of the heirs and is providing information and peace of mind to the survivors.

Although this sounds like a difficult task, it can usually be done easily enough, unless the estate is huge and diverse. A personal representative needs common sense, the services of a competent lawyer, and a willingness to accept responsibility.

The first step in selecting a personal representative is to ask your attorney about the legal limitations. Some states permit only relatives or state residents to act as executors. In other states, there may be no limitation and you can select any individual or institution, or a combination of both.

Here's a checklist of what to look for in choosing an executor:

Ability to get along with your heirs. This applies primarily to your spouse and children. For most individuals, death is a harsh blow. They need support and solace from a person tactful enough to deal with emotional problems, yet strong enough to get the estate settled quickly and fairly.

To make those difficult and sometimes unpopular decisions, empathy on the part of the executor may be especially important when there's a large family. Younger people and nonblood relatives may be viewed with suspicion and older folks may not be able to get along with nonconforming teen-agers. Ideally, the executor should be able to perceive and minimize the effects of such conflicts.

If you do choose a relative, it's a good idea to decide on someone who is not overly involved in family feuds, has tact and concern, and understands your wishes and your family needs.

Ability to command respect. This is an essential requirement if you anticipate controversy among your heirs or business and professional associates or with governmental agencies. Your spouse may not be the best person to deal with your business associates — particularly when the spouse has only known the business associate on a social basis.

Availability. In settling an estate, there are numerous deadlines, documents that require signatures, and occasions calling for personal involvement of the executor. Postponements due to the absence of the personal representative can be costly to the estate, annoying to your heirs, and inconvenient to the lawyer and the court. Choose someone who is readily available and can get the job done.

Executive and administrative ability. The executor is responsible for providing funds for your family and making the best possible arrangements for the disposition of your estate assets. As in the case of choosing a trustee, what you will need in terms of executive and administrative ability depends a great deal on the type of property you own. If you have considerable real estate or substantial security holdings, look for someone with experience in those specific areas.

But don't place more value on this ability than on the ability to maintain good personal relationships, especially when there are young children involved. Extra money is not as important as understanding for your family.

Finally, in choosing an executor, always consider:

Your spouse. If your spouse has been able to handle you (probably her biggest job), manage the household, and bring up the children, she probably has the ability and common sense to retain competent counsel, make proper judgements, and follow the well-established procedures for settling estates.

Outside aid. Again, as in choosing a trustee, whether or not you select a bank or trust company as the executor depends a good deal on the size and complications of your estate. Financial institutions are experienced, efficient, and skilled in handling taxes, estate planning, and investments. But their officers may be impersonal, their policies arbitrary, and their charges too high to be justified except for estates of more than $200,000.

When you consider a lawyer as executor, find one who is experienced in probate, because such expertise can speed settlement and help keep administrative costs low. Experienced lawyers generally do not like to act as executors. They usually do so only in exceptional situations.

In many cases, the best arrangement may be a combination of a relative and a lawyer or institution as coexecutor. Establishing dual responsibility may also be a wise solution. For example, an older sister or aunt might be assigned the care of the children and a bank might handle the money. The disadvantages of such an arrangement are that such split responsibility may be awkward and time-consuming, but it can serve a useful purpose if you have qualms about the management skill of the individual you name as executor.

Before you select a professional fiduciary, discuss the fees, philosophy, and method of operation with a representative of the organization. You can change an executor during your lifetime, but once you die, your will is irrevocable and it is difficult to make a replacement.

To summarize: The choice of your trustee and personal representative should be made on the basis of your family's happiness as well as on business or monetary benefits. You are delegating important authority for the administration of your affairs after you are gone!

10

Sample Plans

The tables you will find in this chapter provide examples of wise estate planning. Rather than describing the needs of particular individuals, they are meant to point out some ways of solving estate planning problems, based on what age group you belong to, the amount of wealth you have, and your family circumstances. As with medical prescriptions, which should not be taken without the advice of a physician, these plans should not be embarked on except with the counsel of a competent attorney.

For each sample we have proposals that, under current laws, appear to be best suited to the manner in which the assets are held. In everyday life, of course, there will be variations in details.

These samples can only be broad guidelines. They do not take into consideration some of the most essential factors in estate planning: your personal and family objectives, your life style, future inheritances, or decisions relating to the choice of a trustee or executor. As already mentioned several times before, successful implementation of every worthwhile estate plan requires frequent review so changes can be made in line with your greater resources, shifting family situations, and new federal and state laws and regulations. For all these reasons, the sample plans that follow are for illustration, not implementation.

YOUNG MARRIEDS

In our experience, Young Marrieds (Table 7) make up the largest single category of persons in need of estate planning. The typical couples we have in mind have been wed about five years and have one or two children. Their income fluctuates, but because they are well trained and educated, they can look forward to ever higher earnings. In the early years, when both husband and wife are working, their income is high. However, it drops a bit when the children come and Mrs. Young Married stays home. Then it moves up again when she goes back to work or the husband gets raises or a better position. The point is that this sample plan is a base and should be reviewed and revised frequently.

Although young couples today may seem to have more material possessions than couples in the past, their net assets are still not large. Homes, cars, furniture, and other possessions can be purchased on credit. The down payments they pay are the minimum. In the first years, therefore, the equity of the Young Marrieds may be low, but this is not a good reason for delaying estate planning, especially when there are children.

Usually, the first step Young Marrieds take in estate planning, in order to create an estate rapidly, is to purchase life insurance. Add the group life policies that come with almost every job today, and they then have a total sum of insurance that puts them at a greater level of wealth than that ever attained by their parents—in our sample (Table 7), an estate of $210,000.

Note that the two major characteristics of the Young Marrieds' estate are that there is very little probate property and that life insurance is the primary asset. Under the Economic Recovery Tax Act of 1981, no federal estate tax is imposed until the adjusted gross estate is over $225,000 in 1982 ($275,000 in 1983; $325,000 in 1984; $400,000 in 1985; $500,000 in 1986; $600,000 in 1987). There could, of course, be state taxes, but generally, if there are any, they would usually be nominal.

The problem that must be provided for is if both parents die. There should be some way of caring for the small children and guaranteeing them the full benefits of their parents' combined estates.

The simplest, best solution would be to set up a two-step arrangement:

1. *Have each estate set up so that if one partner dies, the survivor will receive full rights of ownership of the whole estate.*

This can be done by having the wife named the primary beneficiary of the husband's personal and group insurance ($150,000) and the husband named the beneficiary of her $10,000 group life policy.

All other property can be held in joint tenancy. Probably only in such circumstances would we give such blanket advice about dual ownership. When circumstances change—if greater wealth is obtained through property acquisition, inheritance, more insurance, or raises—a different method of property ownership should be used.

The fact that household goods are not suitable for holding in joint tenancy presents no problem. Most states have a summary procedure (an abbreviated probate process) to assure transfer of such assets to the surviving spouse.

2. *Establish a trust in the will of each parent to take effect only at the death of both parents.* Under this arrangement, all property goes first to the survivor and, at her or his death, to the trust created in the will of the survivor for the benefit of the children. As part of this plan, the contingent beneficiary of all insurance policies should be the trust so that the children will have the protection they deserve, no matter what happens.

Remember, there are extra benefits due from Social security for the widow and children under eighteen (under twenty-two when they are full-time students). The payments will depend on earnings on which social security has been paid and the year of death. When there are two minor children, as in this example, payments could be in excess of $300 per month per child.

Young Marrieds should make a practice of frequently reviewing their estate plans because as circumstances change, adjustments will have to be made. In a surprisingly few years, the family income may increase and debts be paid off, and the estate will be sizable enough to justify revisions of joint tenancy and, possibly, the establishment of trusts to minimize taxes.

Table 7 THE YOUNG MARRIEDS

HUSBAND, WIFE AND TWO MINOR CHILDREN; ANNUAL INCOME $25,000

Life Insurance		
Personal Policy (Mr.'s life)	$100,000	
Group Life (Mr.)	50,000	
(Mrs.)	10,000	$160,000
Homestead (joint tenancy)		
Market Value	80,000	
Less: Mortgage	(45,000)	35,000
Savings and Investments (joint tenancy)	10,000	
Personal Effects	10,000	
Less: Installment Debt	(5,000)	15,000
Total		210,000

DISPOSITION OF ESTATE

Husband's Will   *Wife's Will*

Husband's Will	Wife's Will
1. All my estate to my wife. ⟵⟶	1. All my estate to my husband.
2. If my wife does not survive, then estate goes into trust for children.	2. If my husband does not survive, then estate goes into trust for children.
A. Trustee to provide support and education for children.	A. Trustee to provide support and education for children.
B. When youngest child is 21, divide and distribute the estate equally among children.	B. When youngest child is 21, divide and distribute the estate equally among children.

SINGLES

This important category has its own special estate planning considerations. Members of this group may be delaying marriage, divorced with or without children or some who have chosen not to marry. A significant number live with partners sharing ownership in homes and household goods.

There are several problems encountered by singles which relate more to financial planning than disposition of assets at death. For example, a single cannot depend on a partner's income for support in the event of long-term illness or disability. Acquisition of suitable disability income insurance is a must. Savings for retirement is also important. Even if a participant in an employer sponsored retirement plan, the single should establish an Individual Retirement Account (IRA) and contribute up to $2,000 annually, all of which is tax deductible and which can grow unhampered by income taxes until retirement.

Singles who live with a partner should consult with an attorney regarding the possible use of a written contract. Current legal precedents indicate that a single can expect little or no consideration in the event of a dissolution of the arrangement unless there is something on paper.

A single may elect to have a simple will making outright distributions to various beneficiaries. However, if there are aged parents or young nieces and nephews, the use of a trust should be considered. If the estate is $100,000 or less, it may be best to elect an individual, perhaps a family member, as trustee, avoiding the relatively high minimum fee of a corporate trustee in this situation.

Many states with modern probate codes may allow the testator to have a separate written list of instructions for the distribution of this kind of property which can be changed from time to time without the necessity of amending the will.

Since singles do not have the usual categories of spouse and children as beneficiaries, many consider charitable organizations in their plans.

YOUNG EXECUTIVE

The Young Executive who is depicted in this example (Table 8) is already well on his way to financial success. He earns a good income, considerably above the national average for people of his age, and has more of everything: a homestead that is larger and more costly than that of the Young Marrieds (with a bigger mortgage), outside investments, and more life insurance. His wife is strictly a homemaker and has no separate assets.

The Young Executive puts great emphasis on insurance because of his larger income and because he feels that his family responsibilities are greater than those of the Young Marrieds. In the event of his death, his widow would be under considerable economic strain in order to maintain her standard of living.

Thanks to the policies of his employer, who is anxious to encourage long-term loyalty, the Young Executive has extra benefits:

1. *A $20,000 vested interest in a retirement plan.* This is the dollar value of the savings set aside, in the profit-sharing plan, to finance his ultimate retirement income. This money may not be fully available until the Young Executive decides to retire, but the value may be included in his estate if he dies at an earlier age. The amount of federal and state death taxes, if any, will depend on how the money is paid out at his death. By retirement time, the total will be far greater.

2. *Life insurance of $240,000.* This includes $100,000 personal coverage, $100,000 group insurance, and $50,000 from a specially financed "split-dollar" policy whereby the employer pays that portion of the annual premium that represents the increase in cash value and the employee pays the balance to cover the death benefit cost. Because this arrangement involves borrowing against the cash value of the insurance policy, the net worth of that policy, at the time of this sample plan, is $40,000.

    If the Young Executive should die, there would be two beneficiaries: The company would receive the cash value, and the widow (and/or minor children) would get the much greater death benefit.

Example: For a $50,000 "split-dollar" policy, in the first year, the employer would pay nothing toward the cash value and the executive would pay the entire $1,100 premium (possibly borrowed from the company). In the second year, the policy begins to have a cash value, so the company would pay $240 representing the cash value, and the Young Executive $860 and so on. Soon, the individual's contribution would decrease sharply.

Our Young Executive has a wife and three minor children, currently earns $50,000, owns a total of $240,000 in life insurance, and has a vested retirement benefit of $20,000. He owns a $150,000 house with a $60,000 mortgage, has $45,000 in savings and investments, and personal effects valued at $35,000. In the event of his death, his estate would be $430,000.

The Young Executive's sample plan illustrates the use of two aids in estate planning:

1. A life insurance trust.
2. A pour-over will.

Without the $240,000 in life insurance, the Young Executive's estate is not large enough to justify setting up an *inter vivos* trust. There will be no federal tax because of the marital deduction, unified credit, and expenses. But there may be a small death or inheritance tax imposed in some states.

In terms of taxes, a problem may occur after the death of the survivor, presumably the widow, if the estate exceeds the unified credit. Without proper planning, there may be taxes to be paid.

LIFE INSURANCE TRUST. To deal with such a possibility and also to anticipate greater assets while he is living, the Young Executive should establish a life insurance trust that in the event of the death of the Young Executive would set up two trusts:

1. Trust A, consisting of about $80,000* of his net estate (gross estate less debts and administrative expenses). A formula

---

*Assuming a Unified Credit of $225,000. The Unified Credit increases in a series of steps to $600,000 by 1987.

determines the exact amount so that the Unified Credit and the marital deduction will be used to the best advantage.
2. Trust B, consisting of the remaining assets of the net estate less inheritance taxes, if any.

How the specific assets are divided between the two trusts depends on a number of considerations, including the dictates of federal estate tax regulations and possible future taxes. Generally, however, the allocations will follow the examples described here.

The widow would receive the income from both trusts. She would be able to draw on the principal of Trust A at once, and at her death, could leave the remainder to whomever she named in her will. This provision is called a "general power of appointment." If she does not specify beneficiaries, the balance of the assets of Trust A would pour over into Trust B. It is not necessary to provide your surviving spouse with a general power of appointment. The Young Executive could specifically provide that Trust A on the death of his wife passes to the children in the same way as Trust B. It's a matter of choice.

She is entitled to all the income from Trust B and sums of principal too after the principal of Trust A has been spent and if she needs extra money to maintain her standard of living or for the education of the children. At her death the trust would continue for the benefit of the children. The income and principal would be used for their support and education, and at an appropriate time, the estate would be divided and distributed among them. Principal distributions from Trust B during the wife's lifetime and thereafter for the children would be determined by a corporate trustee.

The date and manner of the ultimate allocation of trust assets could vary according to the wishes of the parents. The terms could be written into the original trust, or the trustee might be given discretionary powers with regard to the allocation.

Some feel that the distribution of assets should be made when the youngest child becomes an adult, at age eighteen, nineteen, or twenty-one, depending on the state of residence. However, our experience has shown that it is better to delay distribution of the principal and, say, give half when each child reaches the age of twenty-five and the balance at thirty.

EMPLOYEE BENEFITS. Retirement benefits must be handled carefully. Federal estate tax law does not permit a lump-sum distribution to avoid death taxes. It is possible to take the money over a period of time in a series of annual payments, but, depending on other factors, such as income taxes, a lump-sum payment may be more advantageous.

An individual who takes early retirement at, say, age sixty-two can take the lump-sum retirement benefit and roll it over into an IRA (Individual Retirement Account). There will be no tax imposed until he withdraws the money.* In the meantime, the executive can take another job, and, in that new position, become a member of another retirement plan with the same tax-deferring benefits. These situations are complex and should be decided upon only after consultation with a tax-knowledgeable lawyer.

The important thing is to stay flexible and consider all the choices. In the sample plan, for instance, the Young Executive should be better off with a lump-sum payment of his retirement benefits at this time. But later, if the value of his retirement fund and his estate grows, another solution might be called for.

WILLS. The Young Executive's will is of the "pour-over" type. His life insurance trust is the pillar of his plan. His personal effects pass to his wife and everything else pours into the life insurance trust, which in turn funnels everything into Trust A and Trust B by a tax-saving formula. (See footnote to Table 8)

As we stress throughout this guide, a wife should make a will of her own. Her assets may be small at the outset, but if her husband dies before her, she will be relatively wealthy. Hers should be a simple will that provides that if she dies first, everything goes outright to her husband. If he dies first, all the property she inherits from him, on her subsequent death, will pour over into the life insurance trust. As a result, after the death of both, all assets would be held in trust for the children and there would be no need to appoint a guardian for their estates to handle any assets.

*He must begin to withdraw funds at age seventy and one-half.

Table 8 YOUNG EXECUTIVE

WIFE AND THREE MINOR CHILDREN; ANNUAL INCOME, $50,000

Life Insurance		
Personal	$100,000	
Split-dollar	50,000	
Minus: Loan	(10,000)	
Group Life	100,000	$240,000
Homestead (joint tenancy)		
Market Value	$150,000	
Less: Mortgage	(60,000)	$90,000
Retirement benefits (vested) in Pension, Profit sharing and Stock-option Plans		20,000
Savings and Investments (own name)		45,000
Personal Effects		35,000
Total		$430,000

Table 8 (continued) DISPOSITION OF ESTATE (death 1982)

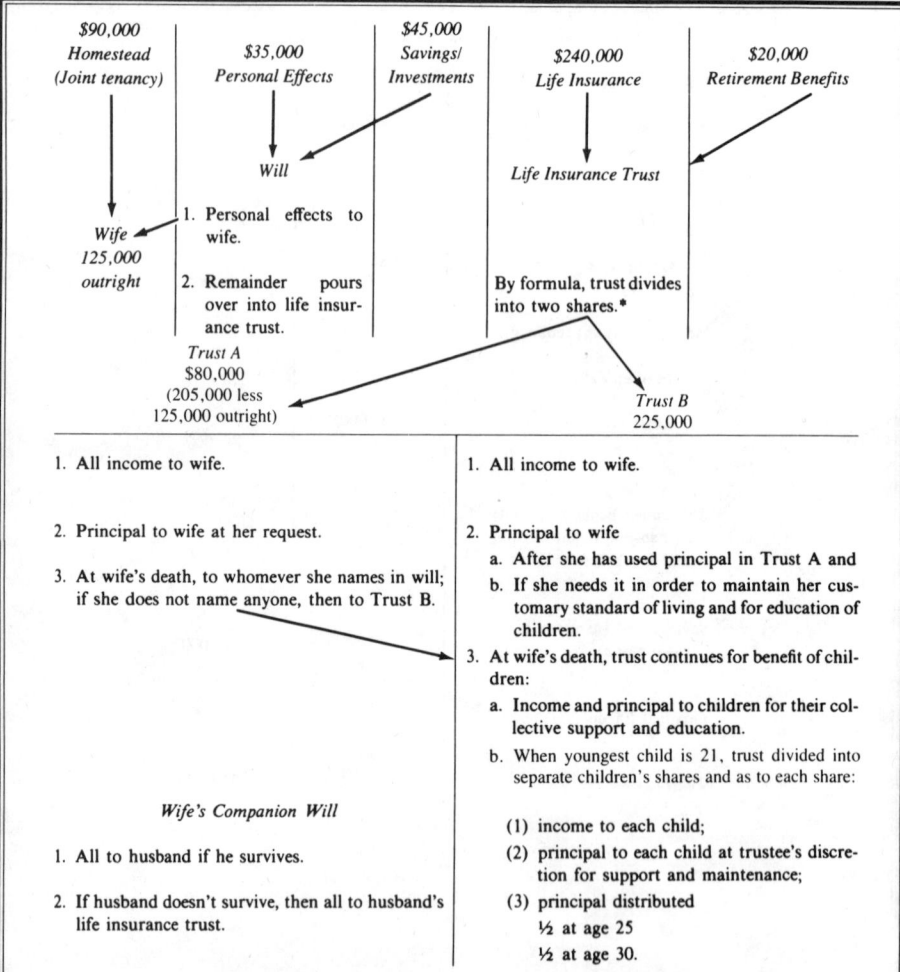

$90,000 Homestead (Joint tenancy)	$35,000 Personal Effects	$45,000 Savings/ Investments	$240,000 Life Insurance	$20,000 Retirement Benefits
↓	↓ Will ↓		↓ Life Insurance Trust	
Wife 125,000 outright	1. Personal effects to wife. 2. Remainder pours over into life insurance trust. Trust A $80,000 (205,000 less 125,000 outright)		By formula, trust divides into two shares.* Trust B 225,000	

1. All income to wife.	1. All income to wife.

2. Principal to wife at her request.	2. Principal to wife
	  a. After she has used principal in Trust A and
	  b. If she needs it in order to maintain her customary standard of living and for education of children.

3. At wife's death, to whomever she names in will; if she does not name anyone, then to Trust B.	3. At wife's death, trust continues for benefit of children:
	  a. Income and principal to children for their collective support and education.
	  b. When youngest child is 21, trust divided into separate children's shares and as to each share:

Wife's Companion Will	(1) income to each child; (2) principal to each child at trustee's discretion for support and maintenance;

1. All to husband if he survives.	(3) principal distributed
	  ½ at age 25
	  ½ at age 30.

2. If husband doesn't survive, then all to husband's life insurance trust.	

*No reduction is shown as a result of expenses for administration, debts, and costs of last illness. All these expenses would reduce Trust B. Usually, provisions are made for all death taxes to be paid in such a manner as to further reduce Trust B. To proceed otherwise would reduce the marital deduction and, in larger estates, would trigger an increase in federal estate taxes.

The formula would be flexible to maximize death-tax savings. Usually it provides that Trust B receive an allocation equal to the amount which is exempt from tax, i.e. exemption equivalent. The remainder would be allocated to Trust A.

INDEPENDENT BUSINESSMAN

The principal asset in the estate of a small businessman (Table 9) is usually his business. The kind of typical businessman depicted in this sample plan has struggled in the early years, been plagued by a shortage of working capital and frustrated by an inability to borrow sufficient funds for needed expansion and updating of equipment. He does not have access to many corporate benefits and, with his limited resources, has been unable to buy as much life insurance as the Young Executive or to set aside, in a retirement plan, as much as the Professional.

His relatively small amount of insurance is often due to distrust of or skepticism about life insurance, which he feels doesn't provide the opportunity for high percentage growth. Such an attitude is unfortunate because the Independent Businessman needs to protect his family and the value of his business after his death.

The Independent Businessman has a wife and three minor children, earns $75,000 a year, and has assets of $585,000: $100,000 in life insurance; a house with a market value of $150,000 (and a $40,000 mortgage); a business with a net worth of about $300,000; $20,000 in retirement benefits; $10,000 in cash (in his own name); investments of $20,000 (securities); and personal effects valued at $25,000.

In planning his estate he should take two steps:

1. *Buy adequate life insurance—about double the $100,000 in the sample.* This will allow his widow to receive support while the executor attempts to get a fair price for the business or to hire a manager until a satisfactory sale can be arranged.

    The estate of $585,000 is adequate except that it lacks liquidity at death. There is relatively little cash and insurance in it. As a result, the well-being of this businessman's family depends a good deal on the sale of the business.

    Small businesses are, characteristically, highly personal affairs. The owner is the chief executive, design engineer, personnel officer, planner, public relations director, and salesman. If he dies before the enterprise has established a firm niche in its field and achieved depth in management,

the value of the company may be difficult to determine and therefore the proceeds of the sale disappointing. When there is just one key man in a business and he dies, it often is difficult for the executor to capture a sale of the business at a fair price. The buyers all try to purchase it at a bargain price.
2. *Groom associates to take over.* If the associates show promise, a purchase and sale agreement (also referred to as a "buy and sell") might be considered. For this plan to work, there must be: (a) a seller who has something to sell and is interested in a sale when certain events (such as disability or death) occur; and (b) a buyer (buyers) who is (are) desirous of purchasing at that time.

A purchase and sale agreement brings buyers and sellers together by providing that in the event of the death of one of them, the survivor or survivors will purchase the decedent's interest. Under such an arrangement, there should always be a definite standard of value for the business. Establishing such a financial point of reference (1) provides protection for the family of the deceased because there is a predetermined method of arriving at a purchase price, and (2) allows the new owner(s) freedom to run the company without interference from the decedent's representative, who, probably, will be inexperienced in the field in which the business operates.

The toughest part of such an agreement is setting the selling price. Formulas are usually inadequate and unsatisfactory. In our experience, it is best to have specific terms, which are mutually agreed upon, reviewed annually, and contain a provision that if the parties fail to agree upon a new value, the old figure will be valid unless it is over two years old. If such terms are not feasible, the agreement should empower a representative of the estate to meet with the purchasers to decide the matter by arbitration if they are unable to agree upon a price.

It is foolish for an Independent Businessman to spend a lifetime building a business and then not be sure of getting adequate value for it in the event of death. That's why we repeat: *For most small enterprises, a purchase and sale agreement is best.*

SAMPLE PLANS

Table 9 THE INDEPENDENT BUSINESSMAN

WIFE AND THREE MINOR CHILDREN; ANNUAL INCOME, $75,000

Life Insurance		$100,000
Homestead (joint tenancy)		
Market Value	$150,000	
Less: Mortgage	(40,000)	
		$110,000
Business		
Book Value	250,000	
Capitalized Earnings*		
$70,000 × 5	350,000	
	600,000	
	(divide by 2)	300,000
Retirement Fund		20,000
Cash (own name)		10,000
Investments		
Stocks and bonds		20,000
Personal Effects		25,000
Total		$585,000

*It is often difficult to determine the value of a small business. In many cases, the value shown on the balance sheet (referred to as "book value" and determined by subtracting liabilities from assets) does not reflect its true value. The earning power of the business might be a better indicator. If the business involves little risk, you might multiply the annual earnings by 6 to 10 times to get a fair figure. On the other hand, if a business is relatively small and risky, a multiple of 5 might be more appropriate. This is the process that is known as capitalization of earnings. In this table, the total of bookvalue and earnings capitalized by 5 is divided by 2.

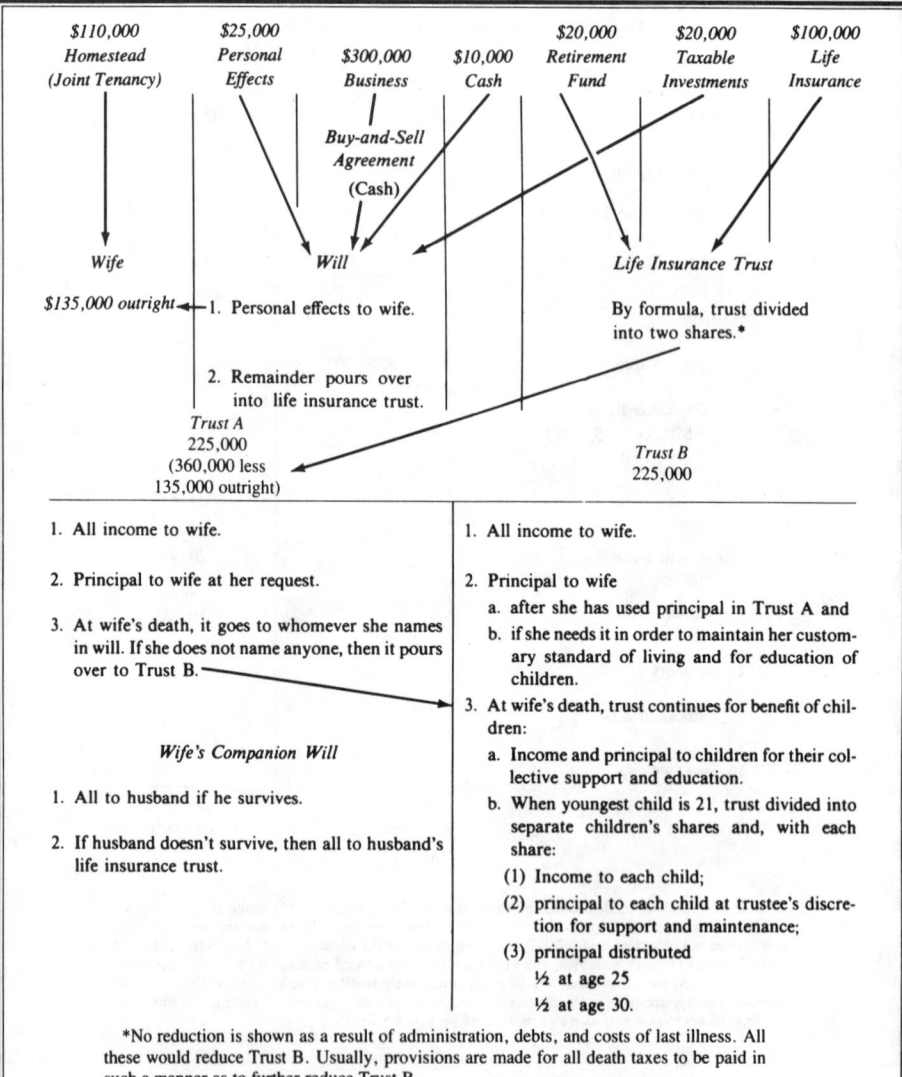

Table 9 (continued) DISPOSITION OF ESTATE (death 1982)

| $110,000 Homestead (Joint Tenancy) | $25,000 Personal Effects | $300,000 Business | $10,000 Cash | $20,000 Retirement Fund | $20,000 Taxable Investments | $100,000 Life Insurance |

Buy-and-Sell Agreement (Cash)

Wife — $135,000 outright

Will
1. Personal effects to wife.
2. Remainder pours over into life insurance trust.

Trust A
225,000
(360,000 less 135,000 outright)

Life Insurance Trust
By formula, trust divided into two shares.*

Trust B
225,000

---

1. All income to wife.

2. Principal to wife at her request.

3. At wife's death, it goes to whomever she names in will. If she does not name anyone, then it pours over to Trust B.

Wife's Companion Will

1. All to husband if he survives.

2. If husband doesn't survive, then all to husband's life insurance trust.

| 1. All income to wife.

2. Principal to wife
   a. after she has used principal in Trust A and
   b. if she needs it in order to maintain her customary standard of living and for education of children.

3. At wife's death, trust continues for benefit of children:
   a. Income and principal to children for their collective support and education.
   b. When youngest child is 21, trust divided into separate children's shares and, with each share:
      (1) Income to each child;
      (2) principal to each child at trustee's discretion for support and maintenance;
      (3) principal distributed
         ½ at age 25
         ½ at age 30.

*No reduction is shown as a result of administration, debts, and costs of last illness. All these would reduce Trust B. Usually, provisions are made for all death taxes to be paid in such a manner as to further reduce Trust B.

The formula would be flexible to maximize death-tax savings. In the settlement of the estate, the $360,000 marital deduction would eliminate federal estate tax (585,000 [Gross Estate] less 225,000 [exemption equivalent for 1982])

The money needed to purchase any small business is hard to come by. There is seldom enough cash in the business to do this and outside financing is usually impossible. The most practical method for obtaining the necessary cash is through insurance on the life of the principal owner. This insurance can be purchased by the owner's business associates directly or through the company, and at the owner's death, the proceeds of the insurance will provide sufficient cash for an outright purchase or, at least, a substantial down payment. At a minimum, the insurance should account for about 30 percent of the purchase price of the business, with the balance to be paid in installments plus interest.

THE PROFESSIONAL

This sample plan is designed to characterize the probable situation of a professional such as a physician, a dentist, a lawyer, or an architect—persons with high recurring incomes. As a rule, such people operate alone or in small groups, are competent in their fields, but often are removed from the details of business and economics. They need counseling and financial planning advice.

The Professional in our sample is married and has three children: a son in medical school, a married daughter with one infant child, and one youngster still at home. He earns a high income, is able to afford a large home, has several different kinds of investments, and uses life insurance as the major source of his estate building. At the point in his career depicted on Table 10, a living trust would be wise. This would save on estate taxes and protect his family. He needs stable assets because, in the past, he has invested in a number of situations, many of which have not fulfilled his expectations.

(Note that a large, ever-increasing portion of his wealth is in his personal retirement plan, which amounts to $100,000 and is growing rapidly as the result of his annual contribution of $15,000 [the maximum for a Keogh plan] plus the reinvestment of income and realized appreciation. In another few years, this fund may be worth substantially more.)

At this time, the Professional's estate totals $975,000: $300,000 in life insurance, $250,000 in homes (in joint tenancy) but subject to a mortgage of 75,000; personal effects of $50,000; $100,000 in a retirement fund; $5,000 cash; investments of $220,000 (in living trust); and $125,000 worth of assets in his practice. His annual income is $130,000: $110,000 earned and $20,000 from interest and dividends.

LIVING TRUST. With such substantial assets, our Professional is ideally situated for setting up a living *(inter vivos)* trust for his investments. As we have seen before, this trust is similiar to a life insurance trust except that it is operative during his lifetime.

The usual provisions of such a trust stipulate that the trustor may deposit in, or withdraw from, the trust whenever he pleases. It is the obligation of the trustee to advise him, from time to time, as to the investment of these funds and, during the course of administration, to account for these investments, to produce records, and to provide information about the taxability of the property in the trust.

In the event of the Professional's death, the trust would operate in exactly the same way as the life insurance trust explained earlier. The life insurance can be made payable to this trust in the same manner as if it were a life insurance trust. This procedure will make it possible to avoid the probate process for all assets that are either already in trust or are payable to a trust by way of a beneficiary designation other than by will.

If the Professional is in partnership or a member of a professional corporation, there should be a buy-and-sell agreement so that the funds tied up in the practice can be obtained quickly after his death.

In the disposition of the Professional's estate, as shown on Table 10, there are two final trusts: Trust A, which takes effect at his death and will total $150,000 after giving effect to the $225,000 (of equity) left outright in the form of the homes held in joint tenancy and the personal effects (the formula in the living trust will carve out the unified credit [$600,000 for those dying after December 31, 1986].

Trust B will receive the balance of $600,000. The decision regarding the allocation of specific assets between Trust A and Trust B is left to the trustee.

Mrs. Professional receives all income of Trust A and B. She can draw on the principal of Trust B after she has used the principal

SAMPLE PLANS

Table 10 THE PROFESSIONAL

WIFE AND THREE CHILDREN: SON IN MEDICAL SCHOOL, MARRIED DAUGHTER WITH ONE INFANT CHILD, AND ONE CHILD AT HOME.

Annual Income	$110,000	
Investment Income	20,000	
Total	$130,000	
Life Insurance		$300,000
Homestead (joint tenancy)		
Market Value	$200,000	
Less: Mortgage	(75,000)	
		125,000
Practice		
Share of equipment	$50,000	
Share of receivables	75,000	
		125,000
Retirement Fund		100,000
Cash		5,000
Investments (own name)		
Savings money market	$60,000	
Mutual Fund Shares	20,000	
Stocks and Bonds	40,000	
Real Estate	80,000	
Royalty Interest (oil)	20,000	
		220,000
Vacation Home (joint tenancy)		50,000
Personal Effects		50,000
Total		$ 975,000

Table 10 (continued) DISPOSITION OF ESTATE (death after 12/31/86)

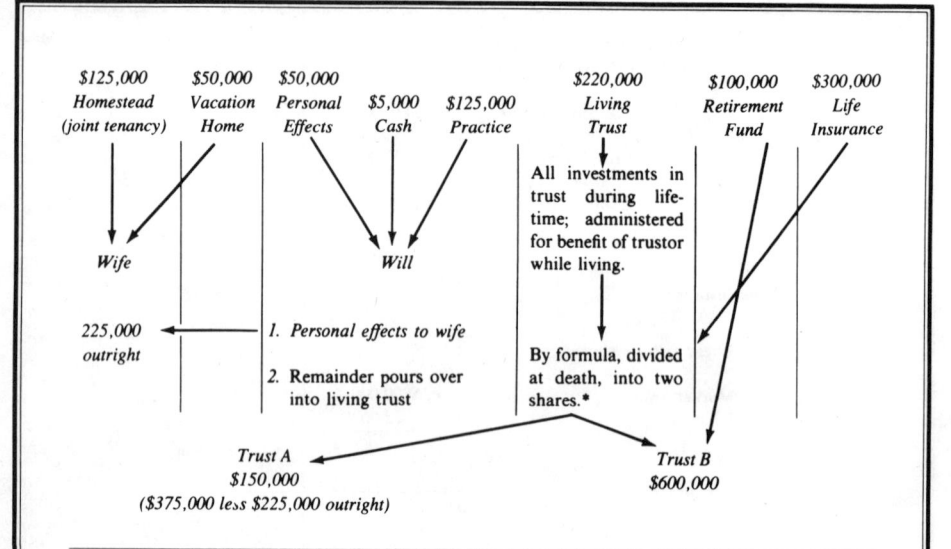

| $125,000 Homestead (joint tenancy) | $50,000 Vacation Home | $50,000 Personal Effects | $5,000 Cash | $125,000 Practice | $220,000 Living Trust | $100,000 Retirement Fund | $300,000 Life Insurance |

↓ Wife
225,000 outright

Will:
1. Personal effects to wife
2. Remainder pours over into living trust

Living Trust: All investments in trust during lifetime; administered for benefit of trustor while living.

By formula, divided at death, into two shares.*

Trust A $150,000 ($375,000 less $225,000 outright)

Trust B $600,000

Trust A

1. All income to wife.

2. Principal to wife at her request.

3. At wife's death, to whomever she names in will. If she does not name anyone, then to Trust B.

Wife's Companion Will

1. All to husband if he survives.

2. If husband doesn't survive, then all to husband's living trust.

Trust B

1. All income to wife.

2. Principal to wife
   a. after she has used principal in Trust A and
   b. if she needs it to maintain customary standard of living and for education of children.

3. At wife's death, trust is divided into three equal parts, each constituting a separate trust as follows:
   a. Income and principal to children for support and education;
   b. distribution of principal to children:
      ⅓ at age 25
      ⅓ at age 30
      ⅓ at age 35.

---

*No reduction is shown as a result of expenses for administration, debts, and costs of last illness. All these would reduce Trust B. Usually, provisions are made for all death taxes to be paid in such a manner as to further reduce Trust B.

*Assuming a unified credit of $600,000 (estates after December 31, 1986) funds in Trust A if she needs additional money to maintain her customary standard of living and to educate the children. At her death, Trust B is divided into three equal parts. The assets will be distributed to the children if they have attained certain ages and if any of them have not attained the prescribed age, that child's share is continued in trust and the trust is administered as follows:

1. Income and principal for support and education.
2. Principal distributed in three payments: one third each time a child reaches the ages of twenty-five, thirty, and thirty-five.

Note that the allocation of trust assets is tailored to the specific needs of the children because of the wide spread in their ages. It would be unwise and possibly unfair to force the oldest child to wait until his young brother becomes an adult. With an estate of this size, early withdrawal of assets will not endanger the economic security of the younger heir.

Let us emphasize again that Table 10 is only a *suggested* plan. Each family has its own set of circumstances and each estate plan should be drafted to meet the family's distinct needs and wishes. Standardized forms and documents won't do the job.

MR. WEALTHY

The sample plan for Mr. Wealthy is more complex than the previous plans and makes use of several trusts (Table 11). The trusts are needed, because: (1) Mr. Wealthy's wife has substantial holdings of her own; (2) his parents need financial help; and (3) much of his estate represents the controlling interest in a business corporation.

Mr. Wealthy is worth $6.5 million, of which $2,500,000 represents control of a closely held corporation. He has a $400,000 mortgage-free home in his own name; $2,300,000 in investments ($1,300,000 in real estate, $600,000 in securities, and $400,000 in cash and equivalents); $600,000 in life insurance; $320,000 in a retirement trust; and $380,000 representing a vacation home, interest in a hunting lodge, country club memberships, and personal effects, including gun and art collections.

Mrs. Wealthy has $500,000 in her own name: $400,000 in inherited securities and $100,000 in jewelry, furs, silver, and other possessions.

Mr. Wealthy's income is $380,000: $200,000 in salary and $180,000 from investments. In addition, his wife gets $30,000 a year from her stocks and bonds. They pay a proportionately high percentage of their income in federal and state income taxes.

The Wealthys have their house in the husband's name.

Mr. Wealthy's personal effects are considerable, so he should make preliminary arrangements for their distribution. He could allocate items with sentimental value in an informal letter or memorandum attached to his will, but larger assets, such as the collections, should be subject to specific instructions to the personal representative (called "executor" in some states) in his will. That's one of the important duties of a personal representative.

Mr. Wealthy's estate plan should make use of trusts in order to avoid or minimize taxes, to retain control of the business, and to be certain that the disposition of the estate will be handled by knowledgeable professionals.

For example, he might use a short-term (Clifford) trust to aid his parents. This would last for their lifetimes or ten years, whichever is shorter. From his ample investments, Mr. Wealthy can afford to divert taxable income to provide financial assistance and economic security for his mother and father. Such an arrangement will reduce the income taxes of the Wealthys, and if his parents do have to pay taxes on their income, the levies will be small by comparison.

Mr. Wealthy is careful about what goes into the trust because he knows that he must give up some measure of control of the assets thus diverted until the death of both parents or until after ten years have passed. He would not want to include any of his business stock, because his lack of control over the property, while it was in the trust, might seriously hamper his administration of the business.

He should consider real estate for insertion in the short-term trust because the management of his real estate, through an agent, would not demand his personal attention or talents. The best property for such a trust would be an income-producing building that has been owned for some time so that its depreciation is no longer much of a factor in reducing Mr. Wealthy's personal income tax liabilities.

SAMPLE PLANS

Because Mr. Wealthy has a considerable number of other assets, and because most of his workday is taken up in the running of his business, he, like Mr. Professional, should take advantage of a living trust (further discussed hereafter).

Before explaining how Mr. Wealthy uses his trusts, let's see whether or not he can benefit from gifts. Until the 1976 Federal Tax Reform Act, wealthy people could reduce death taxes by making lifetime gifts to children and grandchildren. Often, these gifts were made through trusts because the recipients were not considered mature enough to deal with the property at the time of transfer

The old pre-1976 law allowed each gift a $3,000 annual exemption per individual recipient and a $30,000 lifetime exemption for annual gifts in excess of $3,000 per person, and it set gift tax rates at two thirds to three quarters of death tax rates.

But now that there's a unified system, under which gift and death tax rates are the same, and there is no lifetime exemption, there may be little advantage to be gained in making substantial gifts. Three possible avenues for death tax reduction remain:

1. The annual exclusion (increased to $10,000 per year per individual in 1982 and $20,000 if spouse consents) is still available, but if made to a minor, it must come under his control when he becomes of legal age. Longer-term trusts, for example, won't work.
2. Amounts used to pay tuition and medical expenses of, for example, a child or grandchild, are not governed by the $10,000 ceiling and may be paid without limit, free of gift tax.
3. Gifts that are over $10,000 a year may still be worthwhile when the donated property is likely to appreciate in value. The recipient of the gift (donee) gets the giver's (donor's) tax basis. When a gift other than cash is eventually sold, there will be a capital gains tax on all appreciation since the donor's time of purchase.

In making these gifts, Mr. Wealthy will have to recognize the new limitations placed upon lifetime transfers by the unified rate system, as explained above.

Since Mr. Wealthy's business represents a substantial portion of his total estate, and since he has every intention of treating his children equally with regard to the distribution of his estate, he faces an estate planning problem if he wants to assure, as he does, that his oldest son acquires ultimate control of the business. Yet he also wants to make sure that his other children receive an equal share of his estate. One of the solutions available to him is to reorganize or recapitalize his business to produce two kinds of stocks: nonvoting preferred and voting common. The voting common stock will be needed by his son for control of the business. The preferred, which does not enjoy a vote but represents value and will usually pay regular dividends, can be used to equalize the inheritance by passing it to the other children.

Corporate reorganizations and related techniques to transfer control of a substantial corporation to one member of the family and yet treat the other members fairly are beyond the scope of this book. Suffice it to say that such arrangements are usually accomplished during the lifetime of Mr. Wealthy and are quite involved.

Other trusts might include:

1. *An irrevocable life insurance trust* which would care for Mrs. Wealthy and eventually be divided among his heirs could save death taxes.

    The disadvantage in having such a trust is that Mr. Wealthy would lose control of the insurance, which might be useful for collateral in an emergency.

2. *Living trust.* A portion of his investments could be placed in an inter vivos trust. During his lifetime it would be administered, and the income distributed, according to his directions. He would receive income and principal as he requested or needed it. After his death, for example, the assets would be divided into Trusts A and B, all income from Trust A to go to his widow, with principal to be used at her request, and, at her death, to go to whomever she names in her will. If she preferred not to name beneficiaries, the assets of Trust A remaining at her death would go into Trust B.

    Trust B would consist of assets of an amount exempt from federal estate tax. With Trust B, the income might be divided ("sprinkled") among his wife and children according to their relative needs and tax circumstances. Principal could be used for the care and maintenance of Mrs. Wealthy after she has exhausted the liquid principal of Trust A. Principal could also be distributed among children if they needed it, as determined by a corporate trustee. Mrs. Wealthy would also have the power at her death, to allocate Trust B among the children and grandchildren, outright or in continuing trusts. This is referred to as "limited" or "special power of appointment." If Mrs. Wealthy fails to exercise this power, Trust B would continue after Mrs. Wealthy died for the children as shown on Table 11.

3. *Qualified terminable interest property trust* might offer Mr. Wealthy some desired protection for his expanded marital deduction trust. Under the Economic Recovery Tax Act of 1981 the unlimited marital deduction will give Mr. Wealthy's estate a marital deduction for all but $600,000 of the estate (1987 or later death). In this kind of case and in others where the propertied spouse wishes to exert more control over the marital deduction portion, the qualified terminable interest property trust (QTIP) may be the answer. Use of this kind of trust limits the beneficiary spouse to the trust income and does not provide a right to direct the ultimate distribution of trust property remaining at the beneficiary spouse's death, i.e., there is no general power of appointment. Mr. Wealthy could also provide that Trust A assets pass to their children when Mrs. Wealthy dies.

Mrs. Wealthy. If Mrs. Wealthy, who has an estate of her own, dies first, there is little need for her to pass her property on to her husband. He has sufficient wealth and the inheritance would only mean added taxes when he dies. For this reason, it might be wise for Mrs. Wealthy to provide that her estate bypass her husband in favor of her children and grandchildren—or be used in some other way.

If Mr. Wealthy's financial situation were such that he felt he might need his wife's assets, should she predecease him, then her will could leave her assets to him. Mr. Wealthy could then defer a final decision on taking the assets until his wife's death. If he had no need of them, he would disclaim all or part of them and they could go to the children.

For an alternative way to make sure that her husband is never without funds, Mrs. Wealthy could leave her entire estate in a trust that made her husband and the children "sprinkle beneficiaries" of income and principal at the discretion of a disinterested third-party trustee. Mr. Wealthy would never own or control the principal of the trust, so its assets would not be considered part of his taxable estate at his subsequent death.

If Mr. Wealthy dies first, Mrs. Wealthy could also consider:

1. *Leaving everything directly to their children:* She and her husband having worked together in planning their estates, and the distributive provisions of Mr. Wealthy's living trust being agreeable to her, Mrs. Wealthy could provide that all or part of her assets, at her death, pour over into her husband's trust and be allocated according to its terms and conditions.
2. *Leaving all or part of her estate to a trust for the benefit of the grandchildren.* The income and principal would be used for their support and education and the assets divided as each reached maturity, or partially allocated at designated ages.

The Wealthys should consider charities. Gifts to charity can be made directly or retained in trust and parceled out periodically as the trustee sees fit. The easiest and least expensive method is to make outright gifts to charities. But if the Wealthys have a special cause they are interested in, or want to retain greater control over the distributions, they may create a charitable foundation or trust. The foundation can be created during their lifetime or through their wills or trusts. Foundations are for the wealthy. They require considerable thought and professional advice.

As might be expected, the Wealthy family estate plan is much more detailed and diverse than the previous plans. The Wealthys obviously can afford to expend much time and effort on estate planning.

SAMPLE PLANS 117

Table 11 MR. WEALTHY

Family

Son	(33) married, 2 children. Employed in the family business. Father would like to have him run it some day.
Son	(31) married, 2 children. Established physician.
Daughter	(26) married, 1 child. Husband employed by large corporation and family subject to frequent moves.
Son	(17) doesn't know what he wants to do, but leans toward art or other activity allowing him to work with his hands.

Husband's parents are comfortable, but their resources have been depleted by illness.

MR. WEALTHY'S PRESENT ESTATE

Life Insurance		$600,000
Homestead (own name)		
Market Value	$400,000	
Less: Mortgage (none)	0	
		400,000
Investments (own name)		
Stock Portfolio	$300,000	
Municipal Bonds	300,000	
Real Estate (apartment houses)	800,000	
Real Estate (unimproved)	500,000	
Cash and Equivalents	400,000	
		2,300,000
Retirement Fund		320,000
Business Interest (own name, controlling interest in closely held corporation)		2,500,000
Vacation Home (own name)		125,000
Hunting Lodge Interest, Country Club Memberships		25,000
Personal Effects		
Household furnishings and automobiles	100,000	
Gun collection	30,000	
Art collection	100,000	
		230,000
Total		$6,500,000

Table 11 (continued) DISPOSITION OF MR. WEALTHY'S ESTATE (death after 12/31/86)

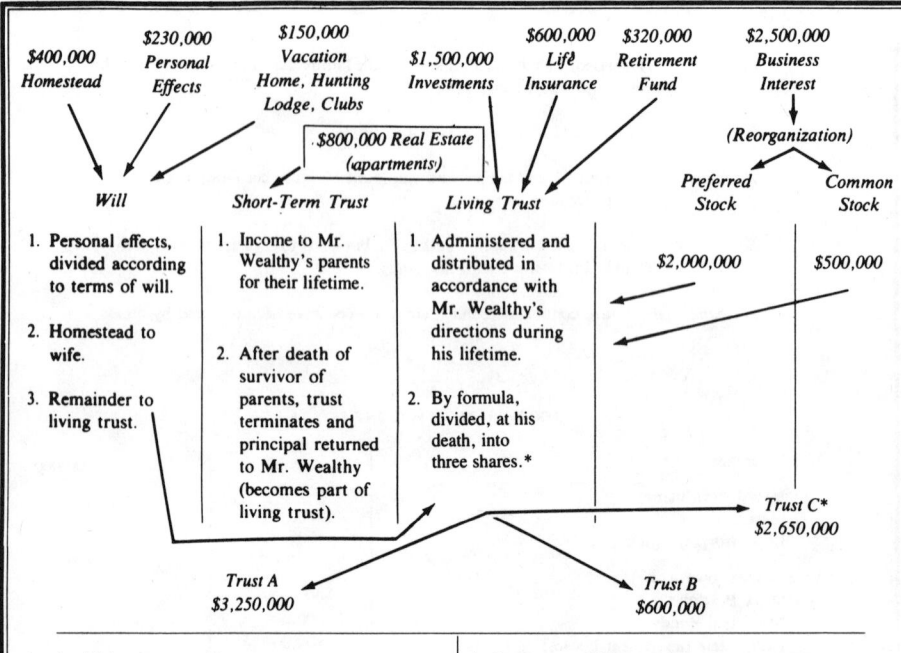

$400,000 Homestead	$230,000 Personal Effects	$150,000 Vacation Home, Hunting Lodge, Clubs	$1,500,000 Investments	$600,000 Life Insurance	$320,000 Retirement Fund	$2,500,000 Business Interest

$800,000 Real Estate (apartments)

(Reorganization) → Preferred Stock / Common Stock

→ Will / Short-Term Trust / Living Stock

Preferred Stock $2,000,000 | Common Stock $500,000

Will
1. Personal effects, divided according to terms of will.
2. Homestead to wife.
3. Remainder to living trust.

Short-Term Trust
1. Income to Mr. Wealthy's parents for their lifetime.
2. After death of survivor of parents, trust terminates and principal returned to Mr. Wealthy (becomes part of living trust).

Living Trust
1. Administered and distributed in accordance with Mr. Wealthy's directions during his lifetime.
2. By formula, divided, at his death, into three shares.*

Trust A $3,250,000

Trust B $600,000

Trust C* $2,650,000

Trust A
1. All income to wife.
2. Principal to wife at her request.
3. At wife's death, trust goes to whomever she names in will. If she does not name anyone, then to Trust B.

*No reduction is shown for expenses of administration, debts, and costs of last illness. All these expenses would reduce Trust B. Usually, provisions are made for all death taxes to be paid in such a manner as to further reduce Trust B.

*Trust C is a qualified terminable interest property trust. It qualifies for the marital deduction in Mr. Wealthy's estate but has provisions identical to Trust B but unlike Trust B, it is subject to tax at Mrs. Wealthy's death.

Trust B / Trust C
1. Income to wife and children as needed, as determined by trustee.
2. Principal to wife for her care and maintenance
   a. after she has exhausted principal of Trust A and
   b. if she needs it in order to maintain her customary standard of living
3. Power in wife at death to allocate among children and grandchildren outright or in continuing trusts.
4. At wife's death if she fails to exercise her power at 3, trust continues for benefit of children:
   a. Income and principal to children for support and education.
   b. When youngest child is 21, trust divided into separate children's shares and, each share:
   (1) income to child;
   (2) principal to child at trustee's discretion for support and maintenance;
   (3) principal distributed
   ½ at age 25
   ½ at age 30.

Table 11 (continued) DISPOSITION OF MRS. WEALTHY'S ESTATE

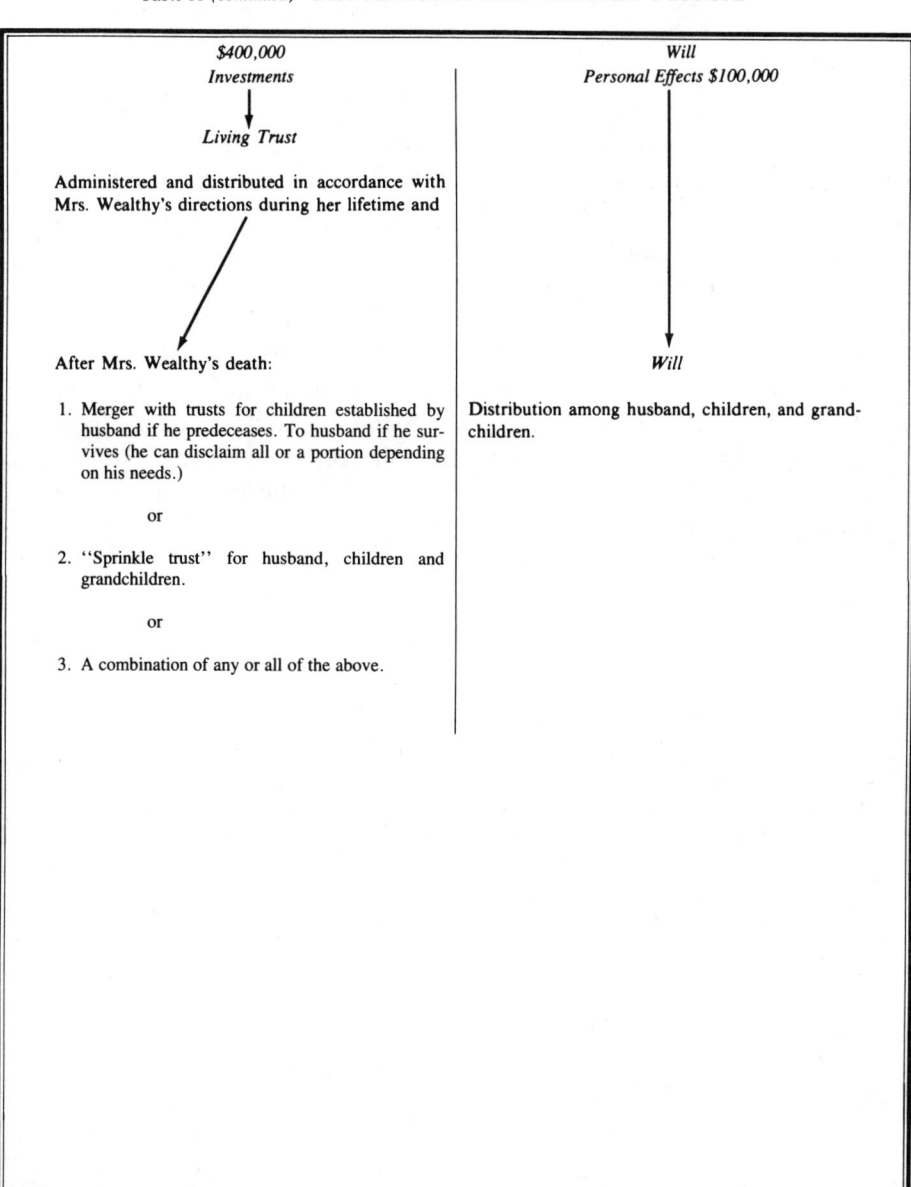

$400,000 Investments	Will Personal Effects $100,000
↓ *Living Trust*	
Administered and distributed in accordance with Mrs. Wealthy's directions during her lifetime and	
After Mrs. Wealthy's death:	Will
1. Merger with trusts for children established by husband if he predeceases. To husband if he survives (he can disclaim all or a portion depending on his needs.)	Distribution among husband, children, and grandchildren.
or	
2. "Sprinkle trust" for husband, children and grandchildren.	
or	
3. A combination of any or all of the above.	

In conclusion

Now you know that there are a number of things you ought to understand in planning your estate. Some of our suggestions and the advice given through the samples will save you money and taxes; other ideas can provide greater security for your loved ones. Taken together, they point the way to a more financially rewarding career while you live and protection for your heirs after you die.

We hope that after reading this guide, you will realize that the single most important action you can take to achieve a useful estate plan is to choose a competent lawyer, and when necessary, other knowledgeable, concerned advisers. Estate planning is too complex and ever-changing to be a do-it-yourself project. One mistake will cost you more, in dollars, inconvenience, and suffering, than the fee for the finest attorney.

INVENTORY 121

ESTATE INFORMATION AND INVENTORY
OF
_____

Date:_____   Telephone:_____
                              Residence:_____
                              Business:_____
                              Social
                              Security
                              No.:_____

I. PERSONAL DATA

                              Known by Any
Your Name:_____   Other Names:_____
Address:_____

                              Vote Where:_____
Auto Tags Where:_____   State Income Tax Paid Where:____
Date of Birth:_____   Place of Birth:_____
Occupation:_____   Annual Income:_____
Date and Place of Marriage:_____
Previous Marriages (how terminated, give name, date and place):_____
_____

State of Health:_____
Spouse -   Known by Any
Full Name:_____   Other Name:_____
Social Security Number:_____
Date of Birth:_____   Place of Birth:_____
Occupation:_____   Annual Income:_____
Previous Marriages (how terminated, give name, date and place):_____
_____

State of Health:_____

Children:

Are any children adopted?_____

Are any children handicapped or in poor health?_____

1. Child's Name:_____ Date of Birth:_____
   Education Completed:_____ If not, Educational Goal_____
   Occupation:_____ Net Worth:_____ Annual Income:_____
   Child's Spouse's Name:_____
   Occupation:_____ Annual Income:_____
   Child's Children:_____ Age:_____
   _____ Age:_____
   _____ Age:_____
   Comments:_____

2. Child's Name:_____ Date of Birth:_____
   Education Completed:_____ If not, Educational Goal_____
   Occupation:_____ Net Worth:_____ Annual Income:_____
   Child's Spouse's Name:_____
   Occupation:_____ Annual Income:_____
   Child's Children:_____ Age:_____
   _____ Age:_____
   _____ Age:_____
   Comments:_____

3. Child's Name:_____ Date of Birth:_____
   Education Completed:_____ If not, Educational Goal_____
   Occupation:_____ Net Worth:_____ Annual Income:_____
   Child's Spouse's Name:_____
   Occupation:_____ Annual Income:_____
   Child's Children:_____ Age:_____
   _____ Age:_____
   _____ Age:_____
   Comments:_____

INVENTORY

Your Parents: Father   *Mother*

Name:_____ _____
Address:_____ _____
Age:_____ _____
State of Health:_____ _____
Financially Dependent?_____ _____

Spouse's Parents:

Name:_____ _____
Address:_____ _____
Age:_____ _____
State of Health:_____ _____
Financially Dependent?_____ _____

       Any Expected Inheritances?   *You*   *Spouse*

From Whom:_____ _____
Approximate Value:_____ _____
From Whom:_____ _____
Approximate Value:_____ _____

Your Brothers and Sisters:

1. Name:_____ Living:_____
   Age:_____ Married:_____ Children:_____
2. Name:_____ Living:_____
   Age:_____ Married:_____ Children:_____
   Comments:_____
3. Name:_____ Living:_____
   Age:_____ Married:_____ Children:_____
   Comments:_____
4. Name:_____ Living:_____
   Age:_____ Married:_____ Children:_____
   Comments:_____

Spouse's Brothers and Sisters:
1. Name:_____ Living:_____
   Age:_____ Married:_____ Children:_____
   Comments:_____
2. Name:_____ Living:_____
   Age:_____ Married:_____ Children:_____
   Comments:_____
3. Name:_____ Living:_____
   Age:_____ Married:_____ Children:_____
   Comments:_____
4. Name:_____ Living:_____
   Age:_____ Married:_____ Children:_____
   Comments:_____

Other relatives or friends of yours and your spouse who you would like to designate as immediate beneficiaries or ultimate beneficiaries if you, your spouse, all issue and parents are dead:

	1.	2.	3.
Name:	_____	_____	_____
Residence:	_____	_____	_____
Age:	_____	_____	_____
Relation:	_____	_____	_____

Charities as immediate beneficiaries or ultimate beneficiaries if all individual beneficiaries are dead:

	1.	2.	3.
Name:	_____	_____	_____
Address:	_____	_____	_____

Armed Forces Service:
Serial No.:_____ Branch of Service:_____
Dates of Service:_____

INVENTORY

II. ASSETS
A. *Bank Accounts and other Cash Resources*

1. a. Name of Bank or Savings and Loan:_____
      Average Balance:_____ Type of Account:_____
      (Checking - Savings)
      In Whose Name (Exact Registration):_____
   b. Name of Bank or Savings and Loan:_____
      Average Balance:_____ Type of Account:_____
      (Checking - Savings)
      In Whose Name (Exact Registration):_____
   c. Name of Bank or Savings and Loan:_____
      Average Balance:_____ Type of Account:_____
      (Checking - Savings)
      In Whose Name (Exact Registration):_____
   d. Name of Bank or Savings and Loan:_____
      Average Balance:_____ Type of Account:_____
      (Checking - Savings)
      In Whose Name (Exact Registration):_____

2. Savings Certificates

In Whose Name (Exact Regis.)	Bank	Rate	Maturity Date	Amount
a.				
b.				
c.				
d.				

3. U.S. Treasury Instruments

In Whose Name (Exact Registration)	Rate	Maturity Date	Amount
a.			
b.			
c.			

4. Other (including Money Market Accounts)

In Whose Name (Exact Registration)	Name of Fund	Amount
a.		
b.		
c.		

B. *Stocks and Bonds*

Number of Shares or Amount	Name of Company	Description of Security	In Whose Name (Exact Regis.)	Present Market Value	Cost	Date of Purchase

C. *Real Estate*

1. Homestead Address:_____
   Brief Description:_____
   _____ Fair Market Value:_____
   Legal Title in Whose Name (Exact Registration):_____
   Mortgage or Contract:_____ Amount:_____
   If Property was a Gift give Donor's cost basis or is in Joint Names indicate contribution of each joint tenant_____

   Cost Information (cost, date of acquisition, cost and date of improvements):_____
   _____

INVENTORY

2. Property Address:_____
   Brief Description:_____
   _____ Fair Market Value:_____
   Legal Title in Whose Name (Exact Registration):_____
   Mortgage or Contract:_____ Amount:_____
   If Property was a Gift or is in Joint Name - Details:_____
   _____

   Cost Information (cost, date of acquisition, cost and date of improvements):_____

3. Property Address:_____
   Brief Description:_____
   _____ Fair Market Value:_____
   Legal Title in Whose Name (Exact Registration):_____
   Mortgage or Contract:_____ Amount:_____
   If Property was a Gift or is in Joint Name - Details:_____
   _____

   Cost Information (cost, date of acquisition, cost and date of improvements):_____

D. *Life and Accidental Death Insurance*

Face Amount	Type	Policy Number	Name of Company	Beneficiaries	Amount of Loan on Policy	Cash Value
1 _____	____	_____	_____	_____	_____	____
2 _____	____	_____	_____	_____	_____	____
3 _____	____	_____	_____	_____	_____	____
4 _____	____	_____	_____	_____	_____	____
5 _____	____	_____	_____	_____	_____	____
6 _____	____	_____	_____	_____	_____	____
7 _____	____	_____	_____	_____	_____	____
8 _____	____	_____	_____	_____	_____	____
9 _____	____	_____	_____	_____	_____	____
10 _____	____	_____	_____	_____	_____	____

Comments on Life Insurance:_____
_____
_____
_____

Is the insured the owner of the policies? If not, give details:_____
_____
_____

E. *Business Interest*

(If you have an interest in a partnership, joint venture, closely held corporation, proprietorship or other similiar entity, the lawyer must have complete information about its assets and liabilities, buy-sell agreements and all other related information including your cost or amount of investment. Attach current balance sheet and profit-loss statement.)

_____
_____
_____
_____
_____
_____
_____
_____
_____
_____
_____
_____

F. *Community Property*

Have you ever lived in a state which has a community property law? (Give name of state and details of any assets acquired).

_____
_____
_____
_____
_____

INVENTORY 129

G. *Pension Plan, Profit-Sharing Plan, Deferred Compensation Agreement, Stock Options, etc.*

Description of Benefits and Values:_____

_____

_____

_____

Beneficiary:_____

_____

H. *Other Assets*

Automobiles (State: Model, Make, Fair Market Value, in Whose Name and Mortgage):_____

_____

Boats, Trailers, etc.:_____

Mortgages Owned, Contracts, Promisory Notes or Other Receivables:_____

_____

China, Silver, Art, Collections, Family Heirlooms:_____

Assets Held as Custodian or as Trustee for Minors or Others:_____

_____

Other Assets (copyrights, patents, options, beneficiary under trust, power of appointment, etc.):_____

_____

_____

III. LIABILITIES

Amount	Owed to Whom	Due Date	Secured by What Asset

Guarantees or Co-Signatures: _____

Other: _____

IV. LOCATION OF CERTIFICATES, DOCUMENTS AND OTHER IMPORTANT PAPERS

Location of Safe Deposit Box: _____
In Whose Name? _____
Any Property of Others in Box? _____ Identifiable as Such? _____
Where are other Valuable Papers Kept? _____

V. SUMMARY

	Husband	Joint	Wife
Assets:			
A. BANK ACCOUNTS AND OTHER CASH RESOURCES	$_____	$_____	$_____
B. STOCKS AND BONDS	$_____	$_____	$_____
C. REAL ESTATE	$_____	$_____	$_____

D. LIFE AND ACCIDENTAL
   DEATH INSURANCE (FACE AMOUNT)

On Husband's Life

Owned by Husband	$_____		
Owned by Wife			$_____

On Wife's Life

Owned by Wife			$_____
Owned by Husband	$_____		
Company Owned	$_____		$_____
E. BUSINESS INTEREST	$_____	$_____	$_____
F. COMMUNITY PROPERTY	$_____	$_____	$_____
G. PENSION PLAN, PROFIT-SHARING PLAN, ETC.	$_____	$_____	$_____
H. OTHER ASSETS	$_____	$_____	$_____
Liabilities (subtract)	$_____	$_____	$_____
TOTAL	$_____	$_____	$_____

VI. MISCELLANEOUS INFORMATION

1. Have you made any substantial gifts in the past or placed property in joint tenancy with a non-contributing joint tenant other than your spouse? If yes, give details._____

_____

2. Do you or your spouse have any powers of appointment? If yes, give details._____

_____

3. Are you or your spouse the beneficiary under any trust? If yes, give details._____

_____

4. Names and addresses of first and second choices for Guardian of the person of minor children, if any.
   First Choice:_____
   _____

   Second Choice:_____

5. Names and addresses of first and second choices for Estate Representative (i.e., Personal Representative or Executor).
   First Choice_____
   _____

   Second choice:_____

6. Do you have any special requests regarding funeral, burial, and donation of body organs (eyes, kidneys, etc.)? If yes, give details._____
   _____
   _____

7. Is there any reason to treat the children other than equally?_____
   _____
   _____

8. Would you like to make gifts of property to children or charities before your death?___
   _____

9. Have you made any agreement to make a Will? Details?_____
   _____

10. Are you party to an Antenuptial (pre-marital) Agreement? If yes, provide a copy.___
    _____

11. Other information you feel is of importance:_____
    _____
    _____
    _____
    _____

Glossary

The following are broad definitions of the words to be found most frequently in trust agreements and wills. Your lawyer can explain the terms in greater detail as the occasion requires.

Assets: What the estate owns: cash, savings accounts, insurance, real estate, stocks and bonds, jewelry, automobiles, furniture, rights to pension plan proceeds, and so on.

Beneficiary: The person designated to receive the income and/or principal of a trust or an estate.

Codicil: An amendment to a will.

Conservator: Same as guardian but person though under disability is not necessarily incompetent.

Corpus: The principal of a fund or an estate, as distinct from interest or income thereon.

Donee: A person to whom a gift is made.

Donor: A person who makes a gift (also called grantor, settlor, trustor).

Estate Planning: The process of planning for the administration and ultimate distribution of one's property. Although usually involving deceased person's property, estate planning can involve the administration of property for a living owner.

Executor: A person or institution named in a will to carry out the instructions of the will. Same as Personal Representative.

Grantor: See Donor.

Guardian: Appointed to protect the assets and person of an incompetent person.

Intestate: To die without a will.

Irrevocable: An arrangement which *cannot* be changed.

Joint-Tenancy: A form of shared ownership where two or more persons own equal interests in certain property and where the surviving joint-tenant or joint-tenants receive title to the property automatically without need for probate.

Life Estate: The right to the use of or income from property during one's lifetime.

Life Tenant: A person holding a life estate.

Non-Probate Estate: Property of a deceased person which passes to beneficiaries or persons sharing ownership in the property and which is not subject to the probate process.

Personal Representative: Same as Executor.

Power of Appointment: Power to name a beneficiary.

Power of Appointment — General: Power without limitation (eg. to anyone including holder of the power).

Power of Appointment — Special: Power limited (eg. to specific persons).

Principal: See Corpus.

Probate: A legal process for determining the instructions of a deceased person regarding his property and seeing that they are carried out.

Probate Court: Jurisdiction over decedents' estates and minors and incompetent persons.

Probate Estate: Property of a deceased person which is subject to probate.

Remainder: The right to property following the death of a life tenant.

Residue: What is left of an estate after specific gifts, administrative expenses, fees and (usually) taxes.

Revocable: An arrangement, such as a trust, which can be changed.

Settlor: See Donor.

Tenancy by the entireties: Special kind of joint tenancy between married persons. Can't be unilaterally severed.

Tenancy in Common: A form of shared ownership where two or more persons own equal interests in certain property and where the interest of the deceased tenant is subject to probate.

Testate: A person who dies with a will. (Intestate = without a will.)

Testator: A person who makes a will.

Trust: A legal entity which is created by the owner of property for the purpose of administering and distributing such property for the benefit of the owner and/or other persons.

Trustee: The individual or organization charged with the management and administration of the assets assigned to a trust.

Trust Fund: A fund, established by trust, for the benefit of an individual or organization.

Trustor: See Donor.

Index

Accountant, 69, 79
Agreements, written, 3, 13, 14, 76. *See also* Partnership; Trusts
Antenuptial agreement. *See* Statutory rights
Assets, 2
  defined, 69
  liquid, readily available, 22
Attorneys,
  role of, 9, 69, 78
  as specialists in probate, 20
  selection of, 80-84

Beneficiary, 69, 70, 72
  designated, 6, 7

Charitable remainder trust, 45
Charitable trust, 44-45
Codicil, 13
Community property states, 5. *See also* Ownership; Property
Conservatorship, 23-24

Donor, defined, 86

Economic Recovery Act of 1981, 28, 51-60, 93, 115

Estate planning,
  figuring net worth, 69, 70, 121-132
  importance of, 1
  for the independent businessman, 103-107
  inventory in, 69, 70, 121-132
  for Mr. Wealthy, 111-115, 117-118
  for Mrs. Wealthy, 115-116, 119
  objectives in, 71-72
  people involved in, 78-79
  for the professional, 107-111
  property and, 2-8
  property in more than one state, 77
  review of, 84-85
  in second marriages, 76-77
  selecting an attorney, 80-82
  setting up a plan, 72-73
  for singles, 75-76
  taxes and, 1
  for unmarried couples, 75-76
  wife's role in, 73-74
  for working spouses, 74-75
  for the young executive, 97-102
  for the young married, 92-95
Executor, 11
  check list for choosing, 89-91
  considerations in choosing, 89-91

defined, 89
Exemption equivalent, 54, 55, 57, 58, 61

Federal Tax Reform Act of 1976, 51, 53, 56, 113

Generation-skipping transfers, 59
Gifts, 116
  taxes on, 29, 49, 56-57
Gift trusts, 44, 116
Grantor. See Donor
Guardianship, 23, 36, 38, 39

Holographic will, 14-15

Income taxes, 41, 45, 47
Inflation, 1
Intangible property, 2
Internal Revenue Service, review by, 62
Inter vivo trust, 24, 43, 75, 108-109, 114-115
Intestate, 18-19
Inventory, 69-70
Investment advisor, 79
IRA, 96, 100
Irrevocable trust, 46, 114

Joint tenancy, 25-33
  advantages of, 26
  decision on use of, 25
  disadvantages of, 27-29
  durable power of attorney, 31-32
  and estate tax savings, 30-31
  limited, 29-30
  Totten trust, 32-33
  and wills, 26, 31

Lawyers. See Attorneys
Life Insurance, 72
  straight, 73
  term, 73
Life insurance agent, 69, 72, 79
Life insurance trust, 98-99, 114
Liquid assets, availability of, 22
Living trust. See Inter vivo trust

Marital deduction, 54, 57, 60

Net worth, figuring of, 69-70
  work sheet, 121-132

Ownership,
  beneficiary designation of property, 6, 7
  community property, 5, 6
  joint tenancy, 4
  partnership, 5
  property held in trust, 7
  property in more than one state, 77
  shared, 3
  shared by agreement, 3
  sole-name, 3
  tenancy by entireties, 5
  tenancy in common, 4

Partnership, 5, 77
Power of attorney, durable, 31-32
Probate,
  defined, 17
  fees, 20-21, 82-84
  length of time for, 19-20
  role of court in, 18-19, 23-24
  tax benefits in, 20
Probate court, role of, 18-19, 23-24
Probate fees, 20-21, 82-84
Property,
  acquisition of, 7
  advantages of trusts in distribution of, 7
  beneficiary designation of, 6-7
  community, 5-6
  held in trust, 7
  intangible, 2
  noncommunity, 5-6
  real estate, 2
  tangible, 2
  types of ownership, 3-7

Qualified terminable interest property trust, 54, 115

Real estate, 2

INDEX

Retirement, 84-85
  benefits, 100
Revocable trust, 46, 114
Right of survivorship, 4

Second marriages, 14, 76
Short-term trust, 47-50
Singles, 75-76
Social security, 84
State taxes, 52-53, 55, 57, 61-62
Statutory rights, 13-14

Tables,
  No. 1 Unified Transfer Tax Rate Schedule-1982, 63
  No. 2 Unified Transfer Tax Rate Schedule-1983, 64
  No. 3 Unified Transfer Tax Rate Schedule-1984, 65
  No. 4 Unified Transfer Tax Rate Schedule-1985 and after, 66
  No. 5 Computation of Maximum Credit for State Death Taxes, 67
  No. 6 Net Federal Estate Tax-1987, 68
  No. 7 Young Marrieds, 95
  No. 8 Young Executive, 101, 102
  No. 9 Independent Businessman, 105, 106
  No. 10 The Professional, 109, 110
  No. 11 Mr. Wealthy, 117, 118, 119
Tangible property, 2
Taxes,
  computation of federal on estates, 51-61, 63-68
  cutting, on death of surviving spouse, 54, 57-59, 60-61
  Economic Recovery Act of 1981, 28, 51-60, 93, 115
  estate, defined, 52
  Federal estate tax laws, 51-61
  Federal Tax Reform Act of 1976, 51, 53, 55, 56, 113
  gift, 29, 49, 56-57
  income, 44-45, 47
  inheritance, defined, 52
  and joint tenancy, 30-31
  marital deduction, 54, 57-59, 60

review by the IRS, 62
  savings in probate, 20
  state, 52, 61-62
  and trusts, 41, 46, 47
Tenancy by entireties, 5
Tenancy in common, 4
Testament. See Wills
Testamentary trust, 42-43
Totten trust, 32-33
Trustee,
  defined, 7, 34-35
  relatives as, 86-88
  remuneration for, 34-35, 87
  responsibilities of, 34-35
Trust officer, 40-41, 69, 79
Trustor. See Donor
Trusts,
  advantages of, 34-41
  charitable, 44-45
  charitable remainder, 45
  college, 48
  cost of setting up, 35
  defined, 7, 34
  generation-skipping, 59
  gift, 44, 116
  income-only, 37-38
  inter vivo, 24, 43, 75, 108-109, 114-115
  life insurance, 43-44
  living, 43, 47-48, 75, 108, 111, 114
  for minor children, 48
  and probate and guardianship, 38-39
  qualified terminable interest property, 54, 115
  revocable and irrevocable, 46, 114
  short-term, 47, 49, 112
  size of, 35
  surviving spouse, 60-61
  and taxes, 41, 60-61
  testamentary, 42

Unified tax credit, 49, 56-57, 98, 113

Vital papers, care of, 22

Wills,
  changing of, 13
  contested as unfair, 12-13

death without (intestate), 18-19
handwritten, 14-15
importance of, 2
invalid, 12
and joint tenancy, 4, 16
periodical review of, 23
pour-over, 100
and probate, 15
residuary clause, 10
safekeeping of, 16
self-prepared, 9
simultaneous death clause, 10-11
statutory rights-premarital agreements, 13-14
tax clause, 11
for unmarried couples, 75-76
valid, 9-11, 18
witnesses to, 11-12